PIEROGI
LOVE

TO PITTSBURGH,
WHICH ALWAYS
HAS MY HEART

First Edition
19 18 17 16 15   5 4 3 2 1

Text and photographs © 2015 by Casey Barber

Published by
Gibbs Smith
P.O. Box 667
Layton, Utah 84041

1.800.835.4993 orders
www.gibbs-smith.com

Designed by Katie Jennings
Printed and bound in Hong Kong

Gibbs Smith books are printed on either recycled,
100% post-consumer waste, FSC-certified papers or on
paper produced from sustainable PEFC-certified forest/
controlled wood source. Learn more at www.pefc.org.

Library of Congress Cataloging-in-Publication Data

Barber, Casey.
  Pierogi love : new takes on an old-world comfort food / written and
photographed by Casey Barber. — First Edition.
      pages cm
  Includes index.
   ISBN 978-1-4236-4065-3
  1. Piroshki. I. Title.
  TX836.B366 2015
  641.81'2—dc23
                2015003933

PIEROGI LOVE

NEW TAKES ON AN OLD-WORLD COMFORT FOOD

WRITTEN AND
PHOTOGRAPHED BY
CASEY BARBER

GIBBS SMITH
TO ENRICH AND INSPIRE HUMANKIND

CONTENTS

INTRODUCTION

Growing up in western Pennsylvania's Allegheny Mountains, my culinary touchstones were as provincial as a city slicker would imagine. Nigiri, tom yum, and injera were completely unfamiliar to me for the first fifteen years of my life. But what I lacked in culinary sophistication, I atoned for with my unintentionally immersive studies in the foods of Pittsburgh's immigrant population: Italian red sauce rich with pork fat; anise-scented pizzelles; kielbasa and sauerkraut bubbling in the Crock-Pot during the holidays; and plates of pierogies at weekend church fairs.

Even if you don't think you know what a pierogi is, chances are you've laid eyes on one at least once in your life. Quite simply, a pierogi is an Eastern European dumpling. A soft but slightly chewy half-moon of dough traditionally filled with potatoes, cheese, meat, sauerkraut, or fruit, then boiled and served with butter, pan-fried onions, or sour cream, a pierogi is its own special breed of comfort food.

The pierogi goes by different names depending on which country it's being eaten in and what it's filled with: Russians, Ukrainians, Hungarians, Czechs, Slovaks, Lithuanians, and Romanians have all historically chowed down on pelmeni, vareniki, varenyky, piroști, or kalduny. Even in Poland, it might be known as a pierogi, pirogi, perogi, perogy, pieroshki, or piroshky. No wonder the uninitiated might be confused—for such a humble food, it gets around.

And though I'll admit we western Pennsylvanians like to think of our region as the epicenter of pierogi pride in America—I mean, the Pittsburgh Pirates *do* have a pierogi mascot race at every home baseball game—we can't take all the credit. From Chicago, which boasts an immigrant history as rich and plentiful as Pittsburgh, to neighborhoods in New Jersey and Brooklyn settled by Slovak and Ukrainian families, to pockets of Polish populations in Wisconsin, Michigan, and even Nebraska, pierogi lovers pop up throughout the United States.

But there's one problem: most people, even ardent pierogi noshers, associate pierogies with old-world sensibilities and peasant food. With this cookbook, I'm rescuing the pierogi from its purgatory in fluorescent-lit, wood-paneled community halls and church basements and bringing it into the modern world. *Pierogi Love* takes that familiar wrapping and stuffs it with a host of unconventional, innovative, and decidedly non-traditional fillings. If Korean BBQ and tacos can happily co-exist, so can Indian rice pudding and Polish dumplings—or French onion soup, for that matter, or Southern pecan pie, or surprisingly elegant rosé-poached pears.

What I'm saying is that you might need to sit your grandma down before showing her this book.

Pierogies are unbelievably versatile and malleable. The modern pierogi is a party host's best friend as a simple freeze-and-serve appetizer; a pop-in-your-mouth game-watching snack that rivals your favorite bar food; a kid-friendly weeknight dinner that boils up in minutes with enough left over for the next day's lunch. It's most definitely dessert, especially when there's caramel and chocolate sauce in the mix. And I'd venture that some of the sweet versions could give donuts a run for their money when there's a deep fryer involved. (Move over, beignets!)

Once you get started, you won't be able to stop the flood of new filling ideas pouring into your brain. Pierogi dough is a blank canvas for whatever you choose to stuff inside—don't stop with the recipes here! I can envision a slew of worldly pierogies, from tikka masala to picadillo. And my jam- and pickle-making friends are already having a field day filling the dough with their own inventive preserves from their pantries.

I hope *Pierogi Love* encourages you to see this classic food in a new light and inspires you to spread the pierogi love in your own lives.

THE BASICS

EQUIPMENT AND INGREDIENTS

You honestly don't need much to make pierogies; after all, cooks around the world have been doing it for centuries without high-tech tools. And while there are molds and presses for assembly line-perfect pierogies, I like to do it the old-fashioned way: by hand. Here's what I use for pierogi-making missions:

NEED-TO-HAVE EQUIPMENT

Mixing bowls: Have at least three, with one bowl big enough to knead in. A stainless steel bowl is key for the chocolate sauces and marshmallow fluff in the Sweet Pierogies chapter.

Rolling pin: Pick one that feels comfortable in your hands; I love the heft of my silicone-coated rolling pin, but plain wood works just as well.

3-inch cookie cutter: Pierogies should be small enough to eat in one or two bites. A 3-inch cutter gives the perfect dough-to-filling ratio without being too small to stuff. (And it's more precise than the Polish grandma method of using an overturned juice glass.)

Rimmed baking sheet: A 9 x 13-inch rimmed baking sheet fits a batch of 24 pierogies snugly and keeps frozen pierogies in place while chilling.

Teaspoon: Though a full complement of measuring spoons comes in handy, the 1-teaspoon measure specifically makes it much easier to get the right amount of filling into each pierogi.

Silicone spatulas: A few quality silicone spatulas (and thicker rounded spoonulas) will serve you well for mixing both dough and fillings.

Small saucepans: A $1^1/2$- to 2-quart high-sided saucepan is the workhorse for most of the fillings in the book, as well as for boiling up to 8 pierogies at a time. A very small 1- or 2-cup saucepan is the perfect size for melting the dough's 3 tablespoons of butter as well as for simmering small amounts of liquid and reheating single servings of chocolate sauce.

Pots for boiling and skillets for frying: For boiling full batches of pierogies, grab a 4-to 6-quart stockpot. You'll also need a good, heavy-bottomed skillet—like a 10-inch cast iron frying pan—for pan-frying pierogies.

Kitchen scale: Trust me when I say a kitchen scale is truly essential and not a fussy tool. It's actually a lifesaver for messy cooks and those who quail at the "exact science" of baking. Dump an ingredient (flour, nuts, cheese, whatever) into a bowl set on the scale; zero the scale out; dump the next ingredient in; repeat. Because everything goes into one bowl, you won't have to search for—or wash—a sinkful of measuring cups, and it's much more accurate to boot!

Every recipe in the book includes weight measurements in ounces and grams as well as volume. Use what you're most comfortable with, but I encourage you to give the kitchen scale a go—OXO and Salter models are affordable and widely available.

Roul'Pat: If you love washable silicone baking sheet liners (AKA Silpats), you'll adore the

Roul'Pat. This large countertop mat provides a smooth, nonstick work surface for rolling out dough, no matter what kind of crappy Formica you might be saddled with.

Bench scraper: Completely optional, but a bench scraper is convenient for dividing dough and transferring chopped ingredients from cutting board to saucepan or bowl. It won't slice through a Roul'Pat like a sharp knife could, and makes picking up sticky bits of scallions or garlic a breeze.

Mini food processor: Because all the filling recipes make small batches (1 to $1^{1}/_{2}$ cups), you'll be dealing with small ingredient quantities. For chopping and grinding, I grab my 3-cup food processor, though the small bowl of a regular food processor works equally well in most cases.

Electric hand mixer: Nope, you don't need a stand mixer for this book. When blending fillings or making homemade marshmallow fluff (page 126), this is all it takes to get the job done.

Candy/oil thermometer: You'll need one for making Caramello pierogies (page 102) or sweet potato pie-rogies (page 124), unless you can accurately determine the temperature of boiling sugar syrup by sight (I know I can't!). Get a dual-read candy and oil thermometer and you might not need that deep fryer I'm about to mention.

Deep fryer: I'm fully aware this is a hard sell. But you haven't lived until you've tasted a truly deep-fried apple pie-rogi (page 87) or crab Rangoon pierogi (page 37). If you don't want to buy an electric fryer, you can use a candy/oil thermometer and a deep, heat-retaining pot like an enameled Dutch oven. I swear it's not as complicated or life-threatening as you think.

INGREDIENTS

Across the board, I subscribe to the ethos that great ingredients guarantee great food. And while I'm all about value, I do recommend a few specific brands for consistent quality and unparalleled flavor:

Valhrona cocoa powder: This fancy French cocoa powder gives cocoa dough (and all your desserts) a richer chocolate flavor than regular Hershey's can offer. If you're feeling flush, you can also use Valhrona baking chocolate in your sauces, though Callebaut or Scharffen Berger baking blocks work well too.

Nielsen-Massey vanilla bean paste: I don't think I exaggerate when I say this stuff is life-changing. It's got the intensely pure flavor of a whole scraped vanilla bean combined with the ease of vanilla extract—you may never return to a regular bottle again.

Flours: For all-purpose and whole-wheat flours, I use King Arthur exclusively—their products have rigorously consistent protein levels that eliminate the chance of ending up with tougher dough in one batch and soft, sticky dough in the next.

For specialty flours in the dough variations on page 17, I've noted my preferences for each.

ASSEMBLING PIEROGIES

TO MAKE 24 PIEROGIES:

Line a rimmed baking sheet with waxed paper or parchment paper.

Divide rested dough into 4 equal pieces with a bench scraper or knife. Set aside 3 dough pieces and cover with the mixing bowl. Roll remaining dough as thinly as possible into a rough 8 x 12-inch rectangle.

Using a 3-inch round cookie cutter, cut out 6 rounds of dough. If the dough isn't quartered evenly, you may get 5 rounds from one piece and 7 from another. Resist the temptation to re-roll dough scraps for additional rounds. It seems wasteful, but the dough won't be as tender the second time around.

Spoon filling into the center of dough rounds. Be judicious with soft fillings like fruit jams—if they spread to dough edges, it will be difficult to pinch shut, so take care not to overfill those varieties!

Using your finger, swipe a *very scant* amount of egg wash—just a light touch—around the dough edge.

Fold into a half-moon shape: Either fold the dough over the filling on the work surface—I call this "the blanket"—or gently cup the pierogi in your hand in a U shape—I call this "the taco."

Gently but firmly seal the pierogi by pinching and squeezing the edges together with your thumb

The Blanket Fold

The Taco Fold

and pointer finger. Start with one pinch at the top, then move to one "corner" of the pierogi and pinch along the edge back to the top. Repeat on the opposite side to finish sealing the pierogi.

Transfer to the baking sheet and repeat with remaining dough rounds and filling.

A NOTE ON FILLINGS:

Each recipe makes enough filling for 24 pierogies, with a few extra spoonfuls for good measure. What to do with leftover filling? Add savory fillings to omelets, use them as sandwich spreads or toppings, or toss with noodles and grains for a quick meal. Swirl sweet fillings into oatmeal, cottage cheese or yogurt, or spoon them on breakfast toast.

COOKING AND STORING PIEROGIES

TO BOIL FRESH OR FROZEN PIEROGIES

Boil a pot of water over medium-high heat (fill approximately 1 quart water for every 6 pierogies). Add pierogies and cook until floating, 2 to 3 minutes for fresh and 4 to 5 minutes for frozen.

TO PAN-FRY FRESH OR BOILED PIEROGIES

Heat 1 tablespoon neutral oil (like canola or vegetable) or melt 1 tablespoon unsalted butter in a skillet over medium heat. Add as many pierogies as will fit in a single layer without crowding. Cook until pierogies are brown and crispy, about 2 minutes per side. Repeat with additional oil or butter and pierogies.

To cook large batches for parties, you can also pan-fry pierogies on an electric or two-burner stovetop griddle.

TO DEEP-FRY FRESH OR FROZEN PIEROGIES

Use an electric deep fryer or a large, high-sided pot filled with at least 2 inches of vegetable or canola oil (fill the pot no more than $1/3$ full). Heat oil to 350 degrees. Add pierogies and cook until golden brown; frying time varies based on equipment, about 3 minutes for fresh and 5 minutes for frozen.

Line a baking sheet with paper towels. Transfer pierogies to the baking sheet and cool for 1 minute.

STORING AND REHEATING PIEROGIES

After making nearly 2000 pierogies for this book (really!), I've come to the conclusion that pierogies are pretty much the perfect make-ahead food. It's so easy to freeze a batch of freshly filled pierogies, then pull out and cook as needed—it's my favorite quick and satisfying meal!

If not freezing or cooking immediately, cover pierogies with plastic wrap or a non-terrycloth kitchen towel, then store at room temperature for 1 hour or refrigerate up to 3 hours before cooking.

TO FREEZE PIEROGIES:

Line a rimmed baking sheet with waxed paper or parchment paper (can be the same sheet as used when assembling pierogies). Place pierogies in a single layer on the sheet and freeze at least 30 minutes or until hard. Transfer frozen pierogies to a zip-top freezer bag or FoodSaver-style bag for vacuum sealing. Store up to 3 months.

TO REHEAT COOKED PIEROGIES:

Reheat pierogies in a 350-degree oven or a skillet over low heat with melted butter or oil, or microwave in 1-minute increments until warm.

Keep large quantities of pierogies warm at parties by tossing with butter or oil and storing in a covered casserole dish in a 300-degree oven.

THE
DOUGH

BASIC PIEROGI DOUGH— SAVORY AND SWEET

Makes enough dough for 24 🥟

2 large eggs

1/2 cup (4 ounces, 113 grams) sour cream or plain Greek yogurt (full-fat, reduced-fat, or nonfat)

3 tablespoons (1 1/2 ounces, 43 grams) unsalted butter, melted and slightly cooled

For savory pierogies: 1 teaspoon kosher salt

For sweet pierogies: 1 tablespoon sugar and 1/4 teaspoon kosher salt

2 cups (8 1/2 ounces, 240 grams) unbleached all-purpose flour

1 tablespoon water

THIS RECIPE IS THE TEMPLATE for every pierogi you'll make in this book, and it's a wonderfully forgiving dough for beginning bakers. There's no finicky yeast to deal with and thus no rising time, just a brief resting period so the flour can become supple and smooth.

If you don't measure your ingredients by weight, it's important to use the spoon-and-sweep method instead of dipping a measuring cup directly into the flour. When you scoop with a measuring cup, the flour is compacted into the cup, adding up to 1 extra ounce of weight (1/4 cup of volume) to each cupful. That translates to too much flour in the dough and tough, chewy pierogies. So either grab a kitchen scale and make life easier, or lightly fluff the flour with a spoon, then use the spoon to fill the measuring cup, leveling excess flour off with a knife.

≫❀≪ ♥ ≫❀≪ ♥ ≫❀≪ ♥ ≫❀≪ ♥ ≫❀≪ ♥ ≫❀≪

Whisk 1 egg, sour cream or yogurt, butter, and salt (for savory pierogies) or sugar and salt (for sweet pierogies) in a bowl. Add flour to a large bowl. Gently stir wet ingredients into flour. The dough will initially be *very* dry and shaggy, seeming as if it will *never* come together, but have no fear: Keep stirring, and it will pull itself into shape.

Once the dough starts to come together, press and smash it against the sides of the bowl with your palms, picking up dough bits and essentially kneading it within the bowl until it forms a ball.

Tip dough and any remaining shaggy flakes out onto a clean work surface or Roul'Pat. Knead until smooth, about 1 minute. Cover dough with the bowl and let rest 15 minutes.

Whisk remaining egg and water in a small bowl for egg wash.

DOUGH VARIATIONS

WHEN YOU WORK WITH THE VARIATIONS that follow below, you'll notice that some doughs don't bounce back as easily as the basic dough does. That's because the gluten content of whole grain flours such as rye or oat is different from all-purpose flour, so you won't get the same amount of stretch.

CORNMEAL

Replace the 2 cups all-purpose flour in the Basic Savory Dough recipe with:

$1^{1}/_2$ cups ($6^{3}/_8$ ounces, 180 grams) unbleached all-purpose flour

$^{1}/_2$ cup (2 ounces, 57 grams) corn flour (Bob's Red Mill)

2 tablespoons (1 ounce, 28 grams) finely ground cornmeal

RYE

Replace the 2 cups all-purpose flour in the Basic Savory Dough recipe with:

1 cup ($4^{1}/_4$ ounces, 120 grams) unbleached all-purpose flour

1 cup ($3^{3}/_4$ ounces, 106 grams) dark rye flour (Bob's Red Mill) or pumpernickel flour (King Arthur Flour)

COCOA

Whisk 2 tablespoons unsweetened cocoa powder into the 2 cups all-purpose flour in the Basic Sweet Dough recipe before adding wet ingredients.

OAT

Replace the 2 cups all-purpose flour in the Basic Sweet Dough recipe with:

1 cup ($4^{1}/_4$ ounces, 120 grams) unbleached all-purpose flour

$1^{1}/_4$ cups (4 ounces, 120 grams) oat flour (Arrowhead Mills or Bob's Red Mill)

WHOLE-WHEAT

Replace the 2 cups all-purpose flour in the Basic Savory or Basic Sweet Dough recipe with:

1 cup ($4^{1}/_4$ ounces, 120 grams) unbleached all-purpose flour

1 cup (4 ounces, 113 grams) whole-wheat flour or white whole-wheat flour (King Arthur Flour)

GNOCCHI DOUGH

Makes enough dough for 24 🥟

1/2 pound (8 ounces, 227 grams) Yukon Gold potato (about 1 medium), chopped into 2-inch pieces

1 tablespoon plus 1 1/2 teaspoons kosher salt

1 1/4 cups (5 1/4 ounces, 150 grams) unbleached all-purpose flour, plus more for kneading and rolling

1/4 teaspoon garlic powder

1 large egg, lightly beaten

THIS DOUGH DIFFERS FROM the preceding variations in that it's essentially a recipe for traditional potato gnocchi, amped up with more flour so it can be rolled out instead of cut into fluffy pasta pillows. Make it immediately before you fill your pierogies, since it doesn't need any resting time and continues to absorb moisture as it sits.

≫❁≪ ♥ ≫❁≪ ♥ ≫❁≪ ♥ ≫❁≪ ♥ ≫❁≪ ♥ ≫❁≪

Place potatoes in a medium saucepan. Add water to cover by 2 inches. Stir in 1 tablespoon salt. Cover and bring to a boil over medium heat. Uncover and cook until potatoes are tender, about 10 minutes. Drain potatoes and return to the pan. Place over low heat and stir for about 30 seconds to remove excess moisture. Run potatoes through a ricer or food mill fitted with fine disk into bowl.

Stir in remaining 1 1/2 teaspoons salt, 1 1/4 cups flour, and garlic powder until mostly combined. Add egg and stir until a sticky dough forms.

Generously flour a clean work surface or Roul'Pat. Using well-floured hands, knead dough until pliant, dusting surface and hands with additional flour as necessary. Divide into 4 pieces and use immediately to make pierogies. Dough will remain soft, so continue to lightly flour work surface and hands as needed to prevent sticking.

SAVORY PIEROGIES

POTATO AND CHEDDAR PIEROGIES
with Caramelized Onions

Makes approximately 24

PIEROGIES

¹/₂ pound (8 ounces, 227 grams) Yukon Gold potatoes (about 1 medium or 2 small), cut into 2-inch pieces

1 tablespoon plus ¹/₄ teaspoon kosher salt

¹/₄ cup (1 ounce, 28 grams) finely shredded Cheddar cheese

1 to 2 tablespoons heavy cream or whole milk

1 batch Basic Savory Dough (page 16)

CARAMELIZED ONIONS

2 tablespoons (1 ounce, 28 grams) unsalted butter

1 large yellow onion halved lengthwise and thinly sliced into strips along the "grain"

¹/₄ cup (or more) chicken or beef broth

Sauerkraut for serving (page 22; optional)

Sour cream for serving (optional)

HOW DO YOU GET a cute, carb-loving, half-Polish guy to marry you? You feed him a batch of homemade potato-cheese pierogies and wait for the proposal in 3 . . . 2 . . . 1 . . .

❧❀❧ ♥ ❧❀❧ ♥ ❧❀❧ ♥ ❧❀❧ ♥ ❧❀❧ ♥ ❧❀❧ ♥ ❧❀❧

FOR PIEROGIES: Place potatoes in a medium saucepan. Add water to cover by 2 inches. Stir in 1 tablespoon salt. Cover and bring to a boil over medium heat. Uncover and cook until potatoes are tender, about 10 minutes. Drain potatoes and return to the pan. Place over low heat and stir for about 30 seconds to remove excess moisture. Run potatoes through a ricer or food mill fitted with fine disk into bowl. Stir in remaining ¹/₄ teaspoon salt, cheese, and 1 tablespoon cream; consistency should be firm enough to roll into a ball. If filling is too dry, stir in additional 1 tablespoon cream.

Roll out dough and stamp into rounds as directed on page 12. Place 1 teaspoon filling on each dough round; brush with egg wash, fold, pinch, and seal as directed.

FOR ONIONS: Melt butter in a medium skillet over low heat. Stir in onion and cook until starting to soften, about 10 minutes. Add ¹/₄ cup broth and bring to a simmer. Cook, stirring occasionally, until onions are very soft and deeply browned, about 1¹/₂ to 2 hours. If onions start to burn before they're fully caramelized, add 1 to 2 tablespoons additional broth as needed.

Deep-fry, boil, and/or pan-fry pierogies as directed on page 13. Serve immediately with caramelized onions, sauerkraut, and/or sour cream.

DO AHEAD: Onions can be made up to 5 days ahead. Cover and refrigerate. Reheat in a skillet over low heat before serving.

SAUERKRAUT PIEROGIES
with Applesauce

Makes approximately 24

PIEROGIES

1 16-ounce bag sauerkraut

1 medium apple, peeled and finely diced

1 small yellow onion, minced

2 to 3 teaspoons sugar

1 batch Basic Savory Dough, Whole-Wheat Dough, Rye Dough, or Gnocchi Dough (pages 16–18)

APPLESAUCE

2 pounds apples (about 5 to 6 medium), peeled, cored, and cut into 1- to 2-inch chunks

$1/4$ cup apple cider or water

1 teaspoon ground cinnamon

$1/4$ teaspoon ground allspice or cloves (optional)

2 tablespoons light or dark brown sugar (optional)

Fresh lemon juice (optional)

THIS RECIPE MAKES MUCH MORE sauerkraut than you'll need to fill the pierogies, but leftovers freeze and thaw easily for future use. Serve the extra with a pork roast or kielbasa on New Year's Day for good luck, as a hot dog topping, or with Reuben sandwiches (or Reuben pierogies, page 38)! You can go with a choice of doughs here: Savory is traditional, Whole-Wheat and Rye are heartier, and Gnocchi lends a delicate potato flavor.

FOR PIEROGIES: Pour sauerkraut and brine into a medium saucepan. Stir in apple, onion, and 2 teaspoons sugar. Cover and bring to a simmer over medium heat. Cook for about 1 hour until the apple and onion are nearly dissolved into the kraut. Add 1 additional teaspoon sugar if the kraut is still too bitter for your taste.

Roll out dough and stamp into rounds as directed on page 12. Place 1 teaspoon filling on each dough round; brush with egg wash, fold, pinch, and seal as directed.

FOR APPLESAUCE: Combine apples and cider or water in a $3^1/2$-quart Dutch oven or heavy pot. Cover, bring to a simmer over medium heat, and cook for about 15 minutes until the apples are very tender, then stir in spices and cook for an additional 5–10 minutes until the apples have broken down into a chunky sauce. Taste and adjust seasoning with sugar and/or lemon juice if desired. (For a smooth sauce, puree with a blender, food processor, or immersion blender.)

Deep-fry, boil, and/or pan-fry pierogies as directed on page 13. Serve immediately with applesauce.

DO AHEAD: Sauerkraut and applesauce can be made up to 1 week ahead. Cover and refrigerate separately.

MUSHROOM PIEROGIES

THOUGH THIS IS ONE OF THE MOST traditional pierogi fillings, my version has a pretty fancy alter ego: it's based on mushroom duxelles, the French way of saying "mushroom stuffing" and a preparation championed by none other than one Ms. Julia Child. This is my way of saying you shouldn't feel weird serving these bites as swanky little canapés!

Melt butter in a large skillet over medium-high heat. Stir in mushrooms, spread in a single layer, and cook without stirring for 5 minutes. Sprinkle with salt and stir to combine. Cook 5 minutes more without stirring; mushrooms should be deeply browned. Add shallot and garlic and cook 3 minutes more. Add wine, stirring to scrape up browned bits, and cook until liquid is mostly absorbed. Add broth and cook until mostly absorbed. Adjust seasoning with additional salt as needed. Transfer to a bowl and cool to room temperature.

Roll out dough and stamp into rounds as directed on page 12. Place 1 teaspoon filling on each dough round; brush with egg wash, fold, pinch and seal as directed.

Deep-fry, boil, and/or pan-fry pierogies as directed on page 13. Serve immediately with sour cream or creme fraiche if desired.

DO AHEAD: Filling can be made up to 3 days ahead. Cover and refrigerate.

Makes approximately 24 🥟

2 tablespoons (1 ounce, 28 grams) unsalted butter

1/2 pound (8 ounces, 227 grams) cremini mushrooms, stemmed, halved crosswise and thinly sliced

1/2 teaspoon kosher salt

1 medium shallot, minced

2 medium garlic cloves, minced

1/4 cup dry white wine

1/4 cup beef or chicken broth

1 batch Basic Savory Dough (page 16)

Sour cream or creme fraiche for serving (optional)

BEEF AND PORK PELMENI
(Russian Pierogies)

Makes approximately 24 🥟

1 tablespoon unsalted butter

1/2 a small yellow onion, minced

1/4 pound (4 ounces, 113 grams) ground beef

1/4 pound (4 ounces, 113 grams) ground pork

1 teaspoon kosher salt

1/2 teaspoon freshly ground pepper

1 batch Basic Savory Dough (page 16)

5 black peppercorns

1 bay leaf

Sour cream for serving (optional)

White wine vinegar or distilled white vinegar for serving (optional)

ACCORDING TO MY FRIEND Irene's mother, who emigrated from the Ukraine in the 1980s, the difference between pelmeni and vareniki or pierogies isn't just the shape (which can be a tortellini-like button or a molded ravioli-like sphere). It's the fact that you're using raw instead of precooked meat for the filling as well. Most Russians don't cook their onions before adding them to the filling, but I love the depth of flavor it adds to the finished product. It's traditional to eat pelmeni with a dollop of sour cream, a splash of vinegar, or both. But since this book is decidedly non-traditional, I say try it however you like it—with vinegar, pan-fried in butter, simply tossed in butter, or even simmered in chicken broth.

❀❤❀❤❀❤❀❤❀❤❀

Melt butter in a small skillet over medium-low heat. Add onion and cook until very soft and starting to brown, stirring frequently, about 10 minutes. Transfer to a bowl and cool to room temperature. Mix the beef, pork, salt, and pepper into onions.

Roll out dough and stamp into rounds as directed on page 12. Place 1 teaspoon filling on each dough round; brush with egg wash, fold, pinch, and seal as directed. To make the traditional pelmeni shape, take the ends of a filled pelmeni and pull them toward each other, bending the half-moon shape until it becomes a round, tortellini-style dumpling. Pinch ends together to seal.

Fill a large pot with water. Add peppercorns and bay leaf and bring to a boil. Add fresh or frozen pelmeni and boil until meat is cooked through, 7 to 8 minutes.

Serve with sour cream and/or splashes of vinegar if desired.

CRAB CAKE PIEROGIES
with Goat Cheese Remoulade

AS A YOUNG EPICURE, I considered crab cakes to be the ne plus ultra of culinary sophistication—which is especially funny when you realize western Pennsylvania is not exactly known for its crustacean population. Growing up, I always ate my jumbo lump-laden cakes from Sunnehanna Country Club or Lombardi's with a simple squeeze of lemon, but these days I'm way into this tangy remoulade. Sub in the pickled celery from page 41 for the pickles or relish if you've got extra around.

>❀≪ ♥ >❀≪ ♥ >❀≪ ♥ >❀≪ ♥ >❀≪ ♥ >❀≪ ♥ >❀≪

FOR PIEROGIES: Combine ¹/₄ cup panko, crab, mayonnaise, mustard, lemon zest and juice, and 1 teaspoon Old Bay in a bowl. Cover and refrigerate at least 1 hour.

Roll out dough and stamp into rounds as directed on page 12. Place 1 teaspoon filling on each dough round; brush with egg wash, fold, pinch, and seal as directed.

If deep-frying pierogies, whisk egg and water in shallow bowl. Place remaining 1 cup panko and remaining ¹/₄ teaspoon Old Bay in a mini food processor and pulse a few times for a slightly finer texture; don't grind down to powder. Pour into another shallow bowl. Dip each fresh or frozen pierogi in egg wash, allowing excess to drip back into bowl, then dredge in panko, shaking off excess. Place on a baking sheet and deep-fry as directed on page 13.

If boiling then pan-frying pierogies, boil until softened, about 2 minutes for fresh or 3 to 4 minutes for frozen. Transfer to a baking sheet until cool enough to handle. Dip and coat pierogies as directed above and pan-fry as directed on page 13.

continued >

Makes approximately 24 🦀

PIEROGIES

¹/₄ cup plus 1 cup panko breadcrumbs

1 cup (6 ounces, 170 grams) crab meat (no need to buy jumbo lump; regular lump, back fin, or claw are fine)

¹/₄ cup (2 ounces, 57 grams) mayonnaise

2 teaspoons coarse Dijon mustard

Zest of 1 lemon

Juice of ¹/₂ lemon

1 teaspoon plus ¹/₄ teaspoon Old Bay seasoning

1 batch Cornmeal Dough or Basic Savory Dough (pages 16–17)

1 egg

1 tablespoon water

REMOULADE

1/2 cup (4 ounces, 113 grams) mayonnaise

2 tablespoons (1 ounce, 28 grams) goat cheese, room temperature

1/4 cup (1 1/2 ounces, 43 grams) finely chopped sweet or dill pickles or relish

1 small shallot, minced

1 medium garlic clove, minced

1 pinch sweet paprika

a few shakes of your favorite hot sauce

FOR REMOULADE: Mix mayonnaise and goat cheese in a bowl, mashing cheese with fork or spatula against side of bowl to remove lumps. Stir in remaining ingredients.

Serve pierogies with remoulade.

DO AHEAD: Filling can be made up to 1 day ahead and remoulade can be made up to 1 week ahead. Cover and refrigerate separately.

SPINACH, HAM, AND GRUYERE
Pierogies with Apple Cider-Braised Leeks

THERE'S BEEN A LITTLE WAR brewing between my husband and me since I started working on this book. Sometimes one of us would get a little attached, shall we say, to a particular pierogi and hoard it for our own snacking purposes. My husband made these disappear so quickly that I didn't even have a chance to fight for them!

≫❁≪ ♥ ≫❁≪ ♥ ≫❁≪ ♥ ≫❁≪ ♥ ≫❁≪ ♥ ≫❁≪

FOR PIEROGIES: Using clean hands, squeeze spinach or press in a mesh strainer to remove as much liquid as possible. Using fingers, fluff spinach so it's not in a tight ball and place in a mini food processor. Add ham and cheese to processor and pulse to finely chop; do not grind to a paste.

Roll out dough and stamp into rounds as directed on page 12. Place 1 teaspoon filling on each dough round; brush with egg wash, fold, pinch, and seal as directed.

FOR LEEKS: Lop off the leek's root and dark green ends and discard. Slice in half lengthwise and briefly soak in a bowl of cool water to remove dirt, then rinse. Slice into $1/4$-inch-thick half moons.

Melt butter in a medium saucepan over medium-low heat. Add leek and apple and cook until leek is very soft, stirring occasionally, about 10 minutes. Stir in the mustard and apple cider and bring to a simmer. Cook until liquid has reduced to a saucy consistency, stirring occasionally, about 20 minutes.

Deep-fry, boil, and/or pan-fry pierogies as directed on page 13. Serve immediately with leeks.

DO AHEAD: Leeks can be made up to 3 days ahead. Cover and refrigerate.

Makes approximately 24 🥟

PIEROGIES

$1/3$ cup (2 ounces, 57 grams) frozen chopped spinach, thawed

$1/8$ pound (2 ounces, 57 grams) sliced deli ham, coarsely chopped (about $1/2$ cup)

$1/4$ cup (1 ounce, 28 grams) shredded Gruyere or Emmenthaler cheese

1 batch Basic Savory Dough or Rye Dough (pages 16–17)

LEEKS

$1/2$ pound leeks (about 1 large or 2 medium)

4 tablespoons (2 ounces, 57 grams) unsalted butter

$1/2$ pound apple (about 1 medium), cut into 3-inch long and $1/4$-inch wide matchsticks

1 tablespoon coarse Dijon mustard

1 cup apple cider

FALAFEL PIEROGIES

Makes approximately 24

1 15-ounce can chickpeas or garbanzo beans, drained but not rinsed

2 tablespoons whole flat-leaf parsley leaves

1 large garlic clove, minced

1/2 teaspoon kosher salt

1/2 teaspoon ground cumin

1/2 teaspoon ground coriander

1/8 teaspoon celery seeds

1 batch Basic Savory Dough (page 16)

1 egg

1 tablespoon water

1 cup whole-wheat breadcrumbs or panko breadcrumbs

EVEN WHEN I WAS a big-shot Manhattan PR girl who got to lunch at DB Bistro Moderne on the regular, I still kept a place in my heart for street-cart falafel. These pierogies are my ode to Rainbow Falafel on 17th Street, incorporating all that irresistibly crispy fried chickpea flavor in dumpling form. Want a dipping sauce? Mix up some tzatziki (page 48).

❀ ♥ ❀ ♥ ❀ ♥ ❀ ♥ ❀ ♥ ❀

Grind chickpeas and next 6 ingredients in a food processor until a chunky paste forms, stopping occasionally to scrape down sides of bowl with spatula. Roll out Basic Savory Dough and stamp into rounds as directed on page 12. Place 1 teaspoon filling on each dough round; brush with egg wash, fold, pinch, and seal as directed.

If deep-frying pierogies, whisk egg and water in shallow bowl. Place whole-wheat breadcrumbs in another shallow bowl. (If using panko, pulse in a mini food processor a few times for a slightly finer texture; don't grind down to powder.) Dip each fresh or frozen pierogi in egg wash, allowing excess to drip back into bowl, then dredge in breadcrumbs, shaking off excess. Place on a baking sheet and deep-fry as directed on page 13.

If boiling then pan-frying pierogies, boil until softened, about 2 minutes for fresh or 3 to 4 minutes for frozen. Transfer to a baking sheet until cool enough to handle. Dip and coat pierogies as directed above and pan-fry as directed on page 13.

DO AHEAD: Filling can be made up to 2 days ahead. Cover and refrigerate.

CELERY ROOT PIEROGIES
with Caramelized Fennel

THE TRADITIONAL PIEROGI PAIRING of potatoes and onions gets a first-class upgrade here, replaced by the subtly sweet and earthy flavors of celery root and fennel. If this is your first time tackling the knobbly celery root, also known as celeriac, go with gusto and you'll be tastefully rewarded.

❧✿❦ ♥ ❧✿❦ ♥ ❧✿❦ ♥ ❧✿❦ ♥ ❧✿❦ ♥ ❧✿❦

FOR PIEROGIES: Slice a piece off top and bottom of celery root so it sits flat on a cutting board. Following the root's curve, slice skin off in pieces from top to bottom. Rinse and cut into 2-inch cubes. Place in a medium saucepan and cover with water. Bring to a boil and cook until tender, about 30 minutes. Drain, then run through a ricer or food mill fitted with fine disk into bowl. Stir in 1 tablespoon cream and salt; consistency should be firm enough to roll into a ball. If filling is too dry, stir in additional 1 tablespoon of cream.

Roll out dough and stamp into rounds as directed on page 12. Place 1 teaspoon filling onto each dough round; brush with egg wash, fold, pinch, and seal as directed.

FOR FENNEL: Trim stems, fronds, and root end off fennel, then slice bulb crosswise into paper-thin slices. Melt butter with olive oil in a medium skillet over medium heat. Stir in fennel and cook, stirring frequently, for 20 to 30 minutes until tender and deep golden brown.

Place caraway seeds in a dry small skillet over medium-low heat. Toast seeds for 1 to 2 minutes until fragrant. Add to fennel.

Deep-fry, boil, and/or pan-fry pierogies as directed on page 13. Serve immediately with fennel.

DO AHEAD: Fennel can be made up to 2 days ahead. Cover and refrigerate. Reheat gently before serving.

Makes approximately 24 🥟

PIEROGIES

1/2 pound (8 ounces, 227 grams) celery root (about 1 small)

1 to 2 tablespoons heavy cream or whole milk

1/4 teaspoon kosher salt

1 batch Basic Savory Dough or Rye Dough (pages 16–17)

FENNEL

3/4 pound fennel (about 1 medium bulb)

2 tablespoons (1 ounce, 28 grams) unsalted butter

1 tablespoon olive oil

1/2 teaspoon caraway seeds

PINK AND PURPLE PRINCESS PIEROGIES

DEPENDING ON YOUR KIDS' PROCLIVITIES, you can either entice them into eating dreaded vegetables with these Crayola-colored pierogies, or blow their little minds entirely. They taste just like regular potato pierogies, but the brilliant pastel tones of these dumplings make them great for princess parties too!

≫✿≪ ♥ ≫✿≪ ♥ ≫✿≪ ♥ ≫✿≪ ♥ ≫✿≪ ♥ ≫✿≪

Place potatoes in a medium saucepan. Add water to cover by 2 inches. Stir in 1 tablespoon salt. Cover and bring to a boil over medium heat. Uncover and cook until potatoes are tender, about 10 minutes. Drain potatoes and return to the pan. Place over low heat and stir for about 30 seconds to remove excess moisture. Run potatoes through a ricer or food mill fitted with fine disk into bowl. Stir in remaining $1/4$ teaspoon salt and 1 tablespoon cream; consistency should be firm enough to roll into a ball. If filling is too dry, stir in additional 1 tablespoon cream.

Make a batch of dough with the following additions: Whisk grated beet in with egg, sour cream, butter, and salt in dough recipe. Add $1/4$ cup flour to 2 cups flour in dough recipe before mixing with wet ingredients.

Roll out dough and stamp into rounds as directed on page 12. Place 1 teaspoon filling on each dough round; brush with egg wash, fold, pinch, and seal as directed. Deep-fry, boil, and/or pan-fry pierogies as directed on page 13, though boiling best retains the dough's pink color.

Makes approximately 24 🥟

$1/2$ pound (8 ounces, 227 grams) purple potatoes, cut into 2-inch pieces

1 tablespoon plus $1/4$ teaspoon kosher salt

1 to 2 tablespoons heavy cream or whole milk

1 batch Basic Savory Dough (page 16)

2 tablespoons finely grated raw red beet (about $1/2$ a small beet)

$1/4$ cup (1 ounce, 28 grams) unbleached all-purpose flour

PEPPERONI ROLL PIEROGIES

Makes approximately 24 🥟

1/2 cup (2 ounces, 57 grams) pepperoni slices, roughly chopped

1/4 cup (1 ounce, 28 grams) finely shredded Italian cheese blend

1 batch Basic Savory Dough (page 16)

2 tablespoons (1/2 ounce, 14 grams) finely grated fresh Parmesan cheese

IN WEST VIRGINIA and western Pennsylvania, pepperoni rolls are almost as revered as pierogies. While some rolls are round and others oblong, and some use pepperoni slices while others use sticks, the basic idea is the same: bread dough and pepperoni baked together for a spicy, greasy treat. Fellow locals might debate the inclusion of cheese here, since it's not always traditional for pepperoni rolls, but it helps bind the filling as the pierogi cooks.

❧❀❦ ♥ ❧❀❦ ♥ ❧❀❦ ♥ ❧❀❦ ♥ ❧❀❦ ♥ ❧❀❦ ♥ ❧❀❦

Pulse pepperoni and Italian cheese in a mini food processor until filling is finely ground but still slightly crumbly.

Roll out dough, whisking Parmesan into flour before kneading. Stamp into rounds as directed on page 12. Place 1 teaspoon filling on each dough round; brush with egg wash, fold, pinch, and seal as directed. Deep-fry, boil, and/or pan-fry pierogies as directed on page 13.

DO AHEAD: Filling can be made up to 3 days ahead. Cover and refrigerate.

SHEPHERD'S PIE-ROGIES

TECHNICALLY, we should only call it shepherd's pie if we're using lamb as the base meat for this comforting wonder; if beef is involved, we should refer to it as cottage pie. Nomenclature lesson aside, this British classic is beloved for its mashed potato topping, so for the pierogi version, it gets wrapped in soft potato gnocchi dough.

Makes approximately 24 🥟

1 tablespoon olive oil

1 large celery stalk, minced

1 small carrot, peeled, minced

$1/4$ a small red onion, minced

2 tablespoons frozen peas

$1/4$ cup dry white wine

1 teaspoon Worcestershire sauce

$1/2$ pound (8 ounces, 227 grams) ground lamb or beef

$1/2$ teaspoon kosher salt

$1/2$ teaspoon freshly ground pepper

1 batch Gnocchi Dough (page 18)

Heat olive oil in a large skillet over medium-low heat. Add celery, carrot, and onion and cook until soft and starting to brown, about 5 minutes. Add peas, wine, and Worcestershire sauce and cook until liquid is mostly absorbed. Transfer to a bowl and cool to room temperature. Mix the meat, salt, and pepper into vegetables.

Roll out Gnocchi Dough and stamp into rounds as directed on page 12. Place 1 teaspoon filling on each dough round; brush with egg wash, fold, pinch, and seal as directed.

Boil fresh or frozen pierogies 7 to 8 minutes to cook meat through, then pan-fry as directed on page 13 if desired. Do not deep fry.

DO AHEAD: Vegetables can be cooked up to 1 day ahead. Cover and refrigerate.

CRAB RANGOON PIEROGIES
with Sweet and Sour Sauce

SINCE WE ALL CAN AGREE that crab Rangoon are the absolute best things (not to mention the most reliable things) on any Chinese takeout menu, I think we all can agree that stuffing pierogies with creamy, salty crab filling is one of the absolute best ideas in finger food history. Deep-fry them to make them as close to authentic crab Rangoon as possible, though you can still boil and pan-fry them if you're a chicken of the sea. Pair these with the pineapple-coconut pierogies (page 99) for a tiki-themed party!

≫✿≪ ♥ ≫✿≪ ♥ ≫✿≪ ♥ ≫✿≪ ♥ ≫✿≪ ♥ ≫✿≪

FOR PIEROGIES: Stir the crab, cream cheese, scallions, and Worcestershire sauce in a bowl until combined.

Roll out dough and stamp into rounds as directed on page 12. Place 1 generous teaspoon filling on each dough round; brush with egg wash, fold, pinch, and seal as directed.

FOR SAUCE: Whisk first 4 ingredients in a small saucepan over medium heat and bring to a simmer. Whisk water and cornstarch in a bowl until cornstarch dissolves. Whisk into saucepan and cook until thickened, stirring constantly, about 1 minute.

Deep-fry, boil, and/or pan-fry pierogies as directed on page 13. Serve immediately with sauce.

DO AHEAD: Filling can be made up to 1 ahead. Sauce can be made up to 1 week ahead. Cover and refrigerate separately.

Makes approximately 24 🥟

PIEROGIES

$2/3$ cup (4 ounces, 113 grams) crab meat (no need to buy jumbo lump; regular lump, back fin, or claw are fine)

$1/4$ cup (2 ounces, 57 grams) cream cheese, room temperature

1 tablespoon minced scallion (about 1 large)

2 shakes Worcestershire sauce

1 batch Basic Savory Dough (page 16)

SAUCE

$1/2$ cup apple juice

2 tablespoons unseasoned rice vinegar

1 tablespoon light brown sugar

$1 1/2$ teaspoons ketchup

1 tablespoon water

$1 1/2$ teaspoons cornstarch

REUBEN PIEROGIES
with Thousand Island Dressing

Makes approximately 24 🥟

PIEROGIES

1/2 cup (3 1/2 ounces, 100 grams) sauerkraut (from recipe on page 22)

1/3 cup (1 1/3 ounces, 37 grams) shredded Swiss cheese, finely chopped

1/8 pound (2 ounces, 57 grams) thinly sliced pastrami, finely chopped (about 1/2 cup)

1 batch Rye Dough (page 17)

1 teaspoon caraway seeds

THOUSAND ISLAND DRESSING

1/2 cup (4 ounces, 113 grams) mayonnaise

3 tablespoons (2 1/4 ounces, 64 grams) ketchup

2 tablespoons (3/4 ounce, 21 grams) sweet pickle relish

1/4 teaspoon Worcestershire sauce

a few shakes of your favorite hot sauce

SINCE THE REUBEN is one of my all-time top five favorite sandwiches, my husband and I have a running joke that I have a Reuben-shaped hole in my stomach: at least once a week, if not more often, I get an intense, all-consuming craving that nothing else can satisfy. I basically have to eat an entire batch of Reuben pierogies to fill the hole, but that's totally acceptable, right?

≫❀≪ ♥ ≫❀≪ ♥ ≫❀≪ ♥ ≫❀≪ ♥ ≫❀≪ ♥ ≫❀≪

FOR PIEROGIES: Mix sauerkraut, cheese, and pastrami in a bowl.

Roll out dough, whisking caraway seeds into flour before kneading. Stamp into rounds as directed on page 12. Place 1 teaspoon filling on each dough round; brush with egg wash, fold, pinch, and seal as directed.

Deep-fry, boil, and/or pan-fry pierogies as directed on page 13.

FOR DRESSING: Stir the ingredients in a small bowl.

DO AHEAD: Dressing can be made up to 1 week ahead. Cover and refrigerate.

BUFFALO CHICKEN PIEROGIES
with Blue Cheese Dip

BUFFALO WINGS are a food I normally associate with football watching and tailgates, not baseball games. But one of my favorite ballpark foods—Citi Field's buffalo dog—is responsible for this pierogi's killer ingredient. The hot dog gets topped with buffalo blue cheese sauce and a blend of shredded pickled carrots and celery, and that hit of vinegar in the pickled vegetables makes all the difference. I might never be able to serve wings the same way again.

FOR PIEROGIES: Whisk vinegar, sugar, and salt in a small bowl until sugar dissolves. Add celery and stir to submerge completely. Let stand at room temperature at least 1 hour.

Melt butter in a small saucepan over medium-low heat, then whisk in the hot sauce to make wing sauce.

Place chicken and 1/4 cup wing sauce in a mini food processor. (Reserve remaining sauce.) Pulse to coarsely chop chicken and blend with sauce; do not grind to a paste. Transfer to a bowl. Drain celery, then stir into filling.

Roll out dough and stamp into rounds as directed on page 12. Place 1 teaspoon filling on each dough round; brush with egg wash, fold, pinch, and seal as directed.

FOR DIP: Whisk sour cream and buttermilk in a small bowl, then stir in the cheese. Refrigerate at least 4 hours or overnight.

Deep-fry, boil, and/or pan-fry pierogies as directed on page 13. Toss with remaining wing sauce if desired. Serve immediately with dip.

DO AHEAD: Filling can be made up to 1 day ahead. Dip can be made up to 3 days ahead. Cover and refrigerate separately.

Makes approximately 24

PIEROGIES

1/4 cup distilled white vinegar

1/4 cup (1³/4 ounces, 50 grams) sugar

1¹/2 teaspoons kosher salt

1 large celery stalk, finely chopped

8 tablespoons (4 ounces, 113 grams) unsalted butter

1/2 cup hot sauce

1/4 pound (4 ounces, 113 grams) shredded cooked chicken breast

1 batch Basic Savory Dough (page 16)

DIP

1/2 cup (4 ounces, 113 grams) sour cream

1/4 cup buttermilk

1 cup (4 ounces, 113 grams) crumbled semi-soft but pungent blue cheese such as Roquefort

SWEET POTATO SAMOSA PIEROGIES
with Apple-Apricot Chutney

Makes approximately 24 🥟

PIEROGIES

1 tablespoon olive oil

1 small yellow onion, minced

2 large garlic cloves, minced

1 teaspoon yellow mustard seeds

3/4 teaspoon kosher salt

1/2 teaspoon curry powder

1/2 teaspoon ground coriander

1/2 teaspoon garam masala

1/4 teaspoon cayenne pepper

1/2 cup (2 1/4 ounces, 64 grams) frozen green peas

1 cup (8 ounces, 227 grams) sweet potato puree

1 batch Basic Savory Dough (page 16)

IF THESE SAMOSA PIEROGIES make you swoon, I can only take credit for having talented friends: This filling comes straight from the kitchen of the incomparable pastry chef (and book recipe tester) Mamata Reddy. Feel free to used canned sweet potato puree here, though you can always roast your own as well.

❖ ♥ ❖ ♥ ❖ ♥ ❖ ♥ ❖ ♥ ❖

FOR PIEROGIES: Heat olive oil in a medium skillet over medium-low heat. Add onion and garlic and cook until onion is soft and just starting to brown, 8 to 10 minutes. Stir in next 6 ingredients and stir for 30 seconds until fragrant. Add peas and cook, stirring occasionally, until completely thawed. Transfer to a bowl and stir in the sweet potato puree.

Roll out dough and stamp into rounds as directed on page 12. Place 1 teaspoon filling on each dough round; brush with egg wash, fold, pinch, and seal as directed.

FOR CHUTNEY: Heat olive oil in a medium skillet over medium heat. Add mustard seeds and cook until starting to pop. Stir in next 4 ingredients and cook until onions start to soften, about 5 minutes. Add apple, apricots, sugar, and vinegar and bring to a simmer, stirring to scrape up browned bits. Cook until the liquid is mostly absorbed, stirring frequently, about 20 to 25 minutes. Transfer to a bowl and cool to room temperature.

Boil, pan fry, and/or deep-fry pierogies as directed on page 13. Serve with chutney.

DO AHEAD: Filling and chutney can be made up to 2 days ahead. Cover and refrigerate separately, and bring chutney to room temperature before serving.

CHUTNEY

1 tablespoon olive oil

1 teaspoon yellow mustard seeds

1 medium yellow or sweet onion, minced

1 tablespoon grated peeled fresh ginger

$1/2$ teaspoon ground allspice or cloves

$1/4$ teaspoon cayenne pepper

$1/4$ teaspoon kosher salt

1 small tart apple, cored and finely diced

$1/3$ cup (2 ounces, 57 grams) finely chopped dried apricots

$2/3$ cup (5 ounces, 142 grams) packed dark brown sugar

$2/3$ cup apple cider vinegar

SANTA FE-ROGIES
with Pico de Gallo

IF YOU'RE NOT USING New Mexico's famed Hatch chiles in this recipe, these pierogies are really just a Southwestern-inspired snack. But I've never met a pun I didn't love, so go ahead and call them Santa Fe-rogies no matter which chiles you use. Go mild or go spicy, it's your call.

FOR PIEROGIES: Heat oil in a medium skillet over medium-low heat. Add onion and garlic and cook until onion is soft and starting to brown, stirring frequently, 8 to 10 minutes. Stir in beans, chiles, and salt and cook until the beans are soft enough to mush with a spatula, stirring occasionally, about 5 minutes. Stir in corn and cooked until warmed through. Transfer to a bowl and cool to room temperature.

Roll out dough and stamp into rounds as directed on page 12. Place 1 teaspoon filling on each dough round; brush with egg wash, fold, pinch, and seal as directed.

FOR PICO DE GALLO: Mix first 5 ingredients in a bowl. Adjust seasoning with more salt and a squeeze of lime juice if desired.

Deep-fry, boil, and/or pan-fry pierogies as directed on page 13. Serve immediately with pico de gallo.

DO AHEAD: Filling can be made up to 3 days ahead. Cover and refrigerate.

Makes approximately 24 🏠

PIEROGIES

1 tablespoon olive oil

1 small yellow onion, minced

1 large garlic clove, minced

1 cup (6 ounces, 170 grams) canned black beans, drained and rinsed

1 4-ounce can chopped green chiles, preferably Hatch

$1/2$ teaspoon kosher salt

$1/4$ cup fresh or frozen corn kernels

1 batch Basic Savory Dough or Cornmeal Dough (pages 16–17)

PICO DE GALLO

$1/2$ pound ripe tomatoes (about 1 large), diced

3 tablespoons (1 ounce, 28 grams) very finely minced red onion (about $1/4$ a small onion)

1 small jalapeño or Serrano chile, stemmed, seeded, and minced

$1/4$ cup minced fresh cilantro leaves and stems

$1/4$ teaspoon kosher salt

1 lime, halved (optional)

GREEK LAMB PIEROGIES
with Tzatziki

Makes approximately 24

PIEROGIES

1 tablespoon olive oil

$1/2$ a medium red onion, minced

1 large garlic clove, minced

2 tablespoons finely crumbled feta cheese

4 oil-cured black olives, pitted and minced

$1/2$ teaspoon freshly ground pepper

$1/4$ teaspoon salt

Zest of 1 small lemon

Juice of 1 small lemon

$1/2$ pound (8 ounces, 227 grams) ground lamb

1 batch Basic Savory Dough (page 16)

TZATZIKI

1 cup ($4^1/2$ ounces, 125 grams) finely diced peeled and seeded cucumber (about 1 small to medium)

1 large garlic clove

Kosher salt

$3/4$ cup (6 ounces, 170 grams) full-fat or reduced-fat Greek yogurt

1 tablespoon minced fresh mint

REPLACE TRADITIONAL PITA BREAD with pierogi dough and you've got a classic Greek meal in appetizer form. I'm a salt fiend, so I pick the briniest olives and feta I can get my hands on for this recipe. If you want to switch it up a bit (or if you're not an olive lover), you can replace the olives with 1 tablespoon rinsed, minced capers.

❦ ❦ ❦ ❦ ❦ ❦ ❦

FOR PIEROGIES: Heat oil in a small skillet over medium-low heat. Add onion and garlic and cook for 8-10 minutes, stirring occasionally, until soft and starting to brown. Transfer to a bowl and cool to room temperature. Stir in next 6 ingredients. Mix lamb into filling.

Roll out dough and stamp into rounds as directed on page 12. Place 1 teaspoon filling on each dough round; brush with egg wash, fold, pinch, and seal as directed.

FOR TZATZIKI: Place diced cucumber and a pinch of salt in a bowl and toss well. Transfer to a strainer and press gently to release any excess liquid. Mince garlic and sprinkle with kosher salt. Press and smear garlic and salt together with the side of your knife, then mince again. Repeat once more. Mix garlic paste with cucumber, yogurt, and mint. Cover and refrigerate at least 1 hour.

Boil fresh or frozen pierogies 7 to 8 minutes to cook meat through, then pan-fry as directed on page 13 if desired. Do not deep fry. Serve immediately with tzatziki.

DO AHEAD: Tzatziki can be made up to 2 days ahead. Cover and refrigerate.

MUSHROOM, GOAT CHEESE, AND CHIVE PIEROGIES

SO YOU'VE MASTERED the art of browning mushrooms for traditional pierogies and want to shake it up a bit . . . may I suggest this dainty little number? Blending meaty mushrooms with soft, tangy goat cheese and a sprinkling of pungent chives makes for a luxurious study in contrast, equally appropriate for a weekend brunch or a midnight snack.

❧❀♥❀❧♥❧❀♥❀❧♥❧❀♥❀❧♥❧❀♥❀❧

Melt butter in a large skillet over medium-high heat. Stir in mushrooms, spread in a single layer, and cook without stirring for 5 minutes. Sprinkle with salt and pepper and stir to combine. Cook 5 minutes more without stirring; mushrooms should be deeply browned. Transfer to a bowl and cool to room temperature.

Transfer mushrooms to a cutting board and finely chop. Return to bowl and stir in goat cheese and chives until blended. Adjust seasoning with additional salt and pepper as needed.

Roll out dough and stamp into rounds as directed on page 12. Place 1 teaspoon filling on each dough round; brush with egg wash, fold, pinch, and seal as directed. Deep-fry, boil, and/or pan-fry pierogies as directed on page 13.

DO AHEAD: Filling can be made up to 1 day ahead. Cover and refrigerate.

Makes approximately 24 🏛

2 tablespoons (1 ounce, 28 grams) unsalted butter

$1/2$ pound (8 ounces, 227 grams) cremini mushrooms, stemmed, halved crosswise and thinly sliced

$1/2$ teaspoon kosher salt

$1/2$ teaspoon freshly ground pepper

$1/4$ cup (2 ounces, 57 grams) goat cheese, room temperature

2 tablespoons minced fresh chives

1 batch Basic Savory Dough or Whole-Wheat Dough (pages 16–17)

BRUSSELS SPROUTS AND BACON PIEROGIES

Makes approximately 24

3/8 pound (6 ounces, 170 grams) Brussels sprouts

3 slices thick-cut bacon, finely chopped

1/2 teaspoon za'atar, or 1/4 teaspoon kosher salt mixed with 1/4 teaspoon dried thyme

1 batch Basic Savory Dough, Whole-Wheat Dough, or Rye Dough (pages 16–17)

SOME PEOPLE CRAVE green bean casserole or scalloped potatoes as their go-to Thanksgiving dish, but I always have a soft spot for shredded Brussels sprouts done up all crispy with flecks of bacon. I can only sneak this side onto the Thanksgiving table once every few years, but with these pierogies, I can get a fix year-round. Za'atar, a tangy Middle Eastern spice blend, gives these a little extra something, but if you don't have it on hand, sub in a simple salt-and-thyme mix.

≫❀≪ ♥ ≫❀≪ ♥ ≫❀≪ ♥ ≫❀≪ ♥ ≫❀≪ ♥ ≫❀≪ ♥ ≫❀≪

Trim roots off Brussels sprouts and finely shred with the slicing disc of a food processor. Or slice each trimmed sprout in half lengthwise and thinly slice by hand.

Cook bacon in a large skillet over medium heat, stirring frequently, until most of the fat is rendered and bacon is crisp. Transfer bacon to a paper towel-lined plate. Leave fat in skillet. Add Brussels sprouts to skillet and cook, stirring occasionally, until sprouts are deep green and beginning to caramelize, about 10 minutes. Stir in za'atar and reserved bacon. Transfer to a bowl and cool to room temperature.

Roll out dough and stamp into rounds as directed on page 12. Place 1 teaspoon filling on each dough round; brush with egg wash, fold, pinch, and seal as directed. Deep-fry, boil, and/or pan-fry pierogies as directed on page 13.

DO AHEAD: Filling can be made up to 2 days ahead. Cover and refrigerate.

SAAG PANEER PIEROGIES

THOUGH I'M ALWAYS drawn to spinach in any dish, I gotta admit that the paneer cheese is my favorite thing about this filling. This fresh Indian cheese is very similar to halloumi and other European "grilling cheeses" that retain their shape when placed over heat. It's widely available at grocery stores and specialty markets, but if you can't find paneer, look for another non-melting cheese.

Grind shallot, chile, garlic, and ginger to a chunky paste in a mini food processor. Heat 1 teaspoon oil in a medium skillet over medium heat. Stir in paste and cook until slightly softened and highly aromatic, about 30 seconds. Stir in spinach, 1/2 teaspoon salt, 1/2 teaspoon garam masala, and turmeric and cook 2 to 3 minutes, stirring frequently, adding 1 to 2 tablespoons of water as needed if spinach sticks to the pan. Transfer to a bowl and cool to room temperature.

Place a paper towel on a plate or cutting board. Whisk flour, remaining 1/4 teaspoon salt, and remaining 1/4 teaspoon garam masala in a bowl. Toss cheese cubes in flour mixture. Transfer to a strainer and shake off excess flour. Heat 1 teaspoon oil in a small skillet over medium heat. Add half the cheese cubes and cook until browned, about 1 minute per side. Drain on paper towel. Repeat with remaining 1 teaspoon oil and remaining cheese cubes.

Roll out dough and stamp into rounds as directed on page 12. Place 1 cheese cube on each round, then top with 1 teaspoon filling; brush with egg wash, fold, pinch, and seal as directed. Deep-fry, boil, and/or pan-fry pierogies as directed on page 13. Serve immediately.

DO AHEAD: Spinach can be made up to 3 days ahead. Cover and refrigerate.

Makes approximately 24 🥟

1 small shallot, coarsely chopped

1 small Serrano chile, stemmed and coarsely chopped

1 small garlic clove, halved

1 half-inch-thick piece fresh ginger, peeled

3 teaspoons vegetable or canola oil, divided

1/4 pound (4 ounces, 113 grams) frozen spinach, thawed and drained

1/2 teaspoon plus 1/4 teaspoon salt

1/2 teaspoon plus 1/4 teaspoon garam masala

1/4 teaspoon turmeric

2 tablespoons unbleached all-purpose flour

1/4 pound (4 ounces, 113 grams) paneer cheese, cut into 1/2-inch cubes

1 batch Basic Savory Dough or Whole-Wheat Dough (pages 16–17)

SALTIMBOCCA PIEROGIES
with Lemony White Wine Sauce

Makes approximately 24

PIEROGIES

1/2 pound (8 ounces, 227 grams) thinly sliced prosciutto, chopped

Zest of 2 small lemons

1 tablespoon minced fresh sage

1 batch Basic Savory Dough (page 16)

SAUCE

1/2 cup dry white wine

1/4 cup fresh lemon juice (from 2 to 3 small to medium lemons)

1/4 cup chicken or vegetable broth

1/4 teaspoon cornstarch

2 tablespoons (1 ounce, 28 grams) unsalted butter

GARNISH

1/4 cup vegetable oil

12–16 small to medium sage leaves

THE TRADITIONAL ROMAN SALTIMBOCCA preparation is to wrap prosciutto slices and sage leaves around a veal cutlet and serve with a buttery wine sauce, but who really needs the cutlet after all? Hey veal, vamoose—you're being taken out of the equation here for a more party-friendly bite.

❀✿❀ ♥ ❀✿❀ ♥ ❀✿❀ ♥ ❀✿❀ ♥ ❀✿❀ ♥ ❀✿❀

FOR PIEROGIES: Mix prosciutto, lemon zest, and sage in a bowl. Roll dough out and stamp into rounds as directed on page 12. Place 1 teaspoon filling on each dough round; brush with egg wash, fold, pinch, and seal as directed.

FOR SAUCE: Bring wine, lemon juice, and broth to a simmer in a small saucepan over medium heat and continue simmering until liquid is reduced by half. Spoon 1 tablespoon of liquid into a bowl and whisk in cornstarch. Whisk butter into sauce until melted, then whisk in diluted cornstarch and cook until sauce has thickened, about 1 minute. Cover to keep warm.

FOR GARNISH: If deep-frying pierogies, fry sage leaves in same oil as dumplings. If not, heat 1/4 cup oil in a small skillet over medium heat until a drop of water flicked into pan sputters on contact. Add sage leaves and cook until color darkens and edges crisp up, about 30 seconds. Remove sage from skillet and drain on paper towels.

Deep-fry, boil, and/or pan-fry pierogies as directed on page 13. Toss pierogies in sauce and serve immediately, garnished with fried sage leaves.

DO AHEAD: Filling can be made 1 day ahead. Cover and refrigerate.

JALAPEÑO POPPER PIEROGIES

Makes approximately 24

2 cups distilled white vinegar

1 cup water

2 tablespoons plus $^1/_2$ teaspoon kosher salt

2 teaspoons sugar

4 medium jalapeño chiles, stemmed and cut into $^1/_8$-inch-thick slices

1 cup (4 ounces, 113 grams) finely shredded Monterey Jack, Cheddar, or block mozzarella cheese (do not use fresh)

$^1/_2$ cup (4 ounces, 113 grams) cream cheese, room temperature

2 tablespoons unbleached all-purpose flour

$^1/_2$ teaspoon garlic powder

$^1/_2$ teaspoon onion powder

1 batch Cornmeal Dough or Basic Savory Dough (pages 16–17)

1 egg

1 tablespoon water

1 cup finely ground cornmeal

I CAN SEE STEELERS FANS across the country going nuts for this unholy combination of everyone's favorite bar bite and every Pittsburgher's favorite dumpling. Fry up a batch for your next tailgate and your friends are going to be pretty damn fanatical.

Bring vinegar, 1 cup water, 2 tablespoons salt, and sugar to a simmer in a medium saucepan over medium heat and stir until sugar and salt dissolve. Add jalapeño slices and simmer until color changes from bright green to dull olive, about 1 minute. Pour into a bowl and let stand 1 hour. Strain, discarding liquid.

Place next 5 ingredients and remaining $^1/_2$ teaspoon salt in a bowl and blend well with a hand-held mixer on medium-low speed. Refrigerate until firm, about 1 hour.

Roll out dough and stamp into rounds as directed on page 12. Place 1 teaspoon filling on each dough round, then top with a pickled jalapeño slice. Brush with egg wash, fold, pinch, and seal as directed.

If deep-frying pierogies, whisk egg and water in shallow bowl. Place cornmeal in another shallow bowl. Dip each fresh or frozen pierogi in egg wash, allowing excess to drip back into bowl, then dredge in cornmeal, shaking off excess. Place on a baking sheet and deep-fry as directed on page 13.

If boiling then pan-frying pierogies, boil until softened, about 2 minutes for fresh or 3 to 4 minutes for frozen. Transfer to a baking sheet until cool enough to handle. Dip and coat pierogies as directed above and pan-fry as directed on page 13.

DO AHEAD: Jalapeños and filling can be made up to 5 days ahead. Cover and refrigerate separately.

PHILLY CHEESESTEAK PIEROGIES
with Provolone Sauce

I LIKE TO THINK OF THIS PIEROGI as a culinary bridge between the western and eastern halves of Pennsylvania: the 'Burgh's beloved snack and the City of Brotherly Love's favorite sandwich, finally living in harmony. We may never stop hating each others' sports teams, but at least we can all get along over dinner.

FOR PIEROGIES: Sprinkle steak slices generously with salt. Heat 1 teaspoon oil in a large skillet over medium-high heat. Add half the steak slices to skillet; do not crowd the pan. Cook until deeply browned, 1 to 2 minutes per side. Transfer to a cutting board and repeat with remaining oil and steak. Add pepper and onion to skillet and cook until soft and caramelized, stirring to scrape up browned bits, about 5 minutes. Chop vegetables and steak together into rough 1/4-inch bits; adjust seasoning with additional salt and pepper if needed. Cool to room temperature.

Roll out dough and stamp into rounds as directed on page 12. Place 1 teaspoon filling on each dough round; brush with egg wash, fold, pinch, and seal as directed.

FOR SAUCE: Whisk first 5 ingredients in a small bowl. Pour milk into a small saucepan and bring to a simmer over medium heat. Add cream cheese cubes, whisking to melt. Whisk in spice mixture and simmer until sauce thickens slightly, about 1 minute. Remove from heat. Add provolone and whisk until smooth.

Deep-fry, boil, and/or pan-fry pierogies as directed on page 13. Serve immediately with sauce, and don't be shy about dipping.

DO AHEAD: Filling can be made up to 1 day ahead and sauce can be made up to 3 days ahead. Cover and refrigerate separately. Reheat sauce over low heat before serving.

Makes approximately 24

PIEROGIES

1/2 pound (8 ounces, 227 grams) rib-eye, top sirloin, flatiron, or hanger steak, trimmed and cut crosswise into 1/2-inch-thick slices

Kosher salt

Vegetable or canola oil

1/2 cup (2 ounces, 57 grams) thinly sliced red bell pepper

1/2 cup (2 ounces, 57 grams) thinly sliced yellow or sweet onion

Freshly ground pepper

1 batch Basic Savory Dough (page 16)

SAUCE

1 teaspoon cornstarch

1/2 teaspoon garlic powder

1/2 teaspoon onion powder

1/2 teaspoon mustard powder

1/2 teaspoon sugar

1 cup whole or reduced-fat milk

1/4 cup (2 ounces, 57 grams) cream cheese, room temperature, cut into 2-inch cubes

1/2 cup (2 ounces, 57 grams) shredded provolone cheese

SHRIMP POTSTICKER PIEROGIES
with Peanut Hoisin Sauce

Makes approximately 24

PIEROGIES

1 tablespoon vegetable or canola oil

1 small shallot, minced

1 large garlic clove, minced

1 half-inch-thick piece ginger, peeled and minced

1¼ cups (2½ ounces, 71 grams) bagged coleslaw mix or 1 cup finely shredded cabbage and ¼ cup finely shredded carrot

½ teaspoon kosher salt

¼ pound (4 ounces, 113 grams) peeled and deveined uncooked shrimp, chopped into large chunks

1 batch Basic Savory Dough (page 16)

SAUCE

3 tablespoons soy sauce

3 tablespoons creamy peanut butter; do not use natural or organic

2 tablespoons packed light brown sugar

1 tablespoon honey

1 tablespoon rice vinegar

1 to 2 teaspoons spicy sesame oil or 1 teaspoon prepared red curry paste (optional)

I fully realize it's basically impossible to quit buying and eating Trader Joe's potstickers—they're sooo tasty and sooo damn convenient. But keeping a frozen stash of these is almost as stress-free as zipping over to TJ's. If you want more of an egg roll effect, take the plunge and deep-fry the pierogies. Keep in mind that because there is raw shrimp in the filling, these pierogies must be cooked thoroughly before serving.

FOR PIEROGIES: Heat oil in a medium skillet over medium heat. Add shallot, garlic, and ginger and cook, stirring frequently, 1 to 2 minutes. Add coleslaw mix and salt and cook until cabbage turns soft and translucent, stirring frequently, 3 to 4 minutes. Transfer to a bowl and cool to room temperature.

Place shrimp in a food processor. Add vegetables and pulse until filling is roughly chopped; do not grind it down to paste.

Roll out dough and stamp into rounds as directed on page 12. Place 1 teaspoon filling on each dough round; brush with egg wash, fold, pinch, and seal as directed.

FOR SAUCE: Whisk first 5 ingredients in a small bowl. For spicy sauce, whisk in sesame oil or curry paste. Let stand until ready to use.

Deep-fry fresh or frozen pierogies 5 to 6 minutes as directed on page 13. Alternatively, boil fresh or frozen pierogies 7 to 8 minutes, then pan-fry if desired. Serve immediately with sauce.

DO AHEAD: Shrimp filling can be made up to 4 hours ahead. Sauce can be made up to 1 week ahead. Cover and refrigerate separately.

JALAPEÑO MAC AND CHEESE PIEROGIES

EVERY SPORTS BAR worth its salt has fried mac and cheese bites on its menu these days—who's to say mac and cheese pierogies won't be the next big thing? Even if you think you don't like spicy food, I encourage you to use the jalapeño; its heat is subtle and its flavor really makes the filling pop.

Heat oil in a large skillet over medium heat. Add shallot, jalapeño, garlic, and salt and cook until softened, stirring frequently, 5 to 8 minutes. Stir in 1 cup milk and bring to a simmer. Add pasta and cook until al dente and most of the milk has been absorbed, stirring frequently, about 20 minutes. (If pasta is absorbing milk too quickly, reduce heat to low and stir in more milk $^{1}/_{4}$ cup at a time.) Remove pan from heat. Add cheeses and stir until melted.

Roll out dough and stamp into rounds as directed on page 12. Place 1 teaspoon filling on each dough round; brush with egg wash, fold, pinch, and seal as directed.

If deep-frying pierogies, whisk egg and water in shallow bowl. Pulse panko in a mini food processor a few times for a slightly finer texture; don't grind down to powder. Pour into another shallow bowl. Dip each fresh or frozen pierogi in egg wash, allowing excess to drip back into bowl, then dredge in panko, shaking off excess. Place on baking sheet and deep-fry as directed on page 13.

If boiling then pan-frying pierogies, boil until softened, about 2 minutes for fresh or 3 to 4 minutes for frozen. Transfer to a baking sheet until cool enough to handle. Dip and coat pierogies as directed above and pan-fry as directed on page 13.

DO AHEAD: Filling can be made up to 1 day ahead, though it will be much less creamy than if used immediately. Cover and refrigerate.

Makes approximately 24

1 tablespoon olive oil

1 small shallot, minced

1 small jalapeño chile, stemmed, seeded, and minced

1 medium garlic clove, minced

$^{1}/_{4}$ teaspoon salt

1 cup (or more) whole or reduced-fat milk

$^{1}/_{2}$ cup (2 ounces, 57 grams) ditalini or elbow pasta

$^{1}/_{4}$ cup (1 ounce, 28 grams) shredded fontina or Monterey jack cheese

$^{1}/_{4}$ cup (1 ounce, 28 grams) shredded sharp Cheddar cheese

1 batch Basic Savory Dough or Cornmeal Dough (pages 16–17)

1 egg

1 tablespoon water

1 cup panko breadcrumbs

MAPLE BREAKFAST SAUSAGE PIEROGIES

Makes approximately 24

1 tablespoon olive oil

1 small shallot, minced

1 teaspoon minced fresh sage

1 teaspoon whole fennel seeds

$^1/_2$ teaspoon kosher salt

$^1/_4$ teaspoon freshly ground pepper

$^1/_4$ teaspoon crushed red pepper flakes

1 tablespoon dark maple syrup

$^1/_2$ pound (8 ounces, 227 grams) ground pork

1 batch Basic Savory Dough, Whole-Wheat Dough, Basic Sweet Dough, or Oat Dough (pages 16–17)

Additional maple syrup for serving (optional)

IF YOU'RE THE KIND OF PERSON who forks up stacks of pancakes and sausage to get the most sweet-and-savory bang for your buck, you'll go hog wild over these maple sausage-filled bites. If you're the weirdo who creates waffle dams to keep syrup from touching your breakfast meats, well, I can't help you here. Choose your dough based on whether you'd rather accentuate the sweet or savory side of these pierogies.

Heat oil in a medium skillet over medium-high heat. Add shallot and cook until soft and starting to brown, stirring frequently, about 3 minutes. Stir in next 5 ingredients and cook until fragrant, stirring frequently, about 2 minutes. Transfer to a bowl and stir in maple syrup. Cool to room temperature.

Mix the pork into shallot mixture.

Roll out dough and stamp into rounds as directed on page 12. Place 1 teaspoon filling on each dough round; brush with egg wash, fold, pinch, and seal as directed.

Boil pierogies to cook meat through, 7 to 8 minutes, then pan-fry as directed on page 13 if desired. Do not deep fry. Serve with additional maple syrup.

DO AHEAD: Shallot mixture can be made up to 1 day ahead. Cover and refrigerate.

CHEESY PRETZEL PIEROGIES

NORMALLY, I'd never suggest baking a pierogi—the dough doesn't typically do well in dry heat—but there's no way to get a pretzel's perfect brown finish without some oven time. Luckily, there's also no way to make a pretzel without dunking it in a baking soda solution, which not only creates that glossy exterior but also insulates the pierogi as it bakes. It's funny how perfectly things work out!

Preheat oven to 375 degrees. Line a baking sheet with parchment paper or a silicone liner. Add first 5 ingredients to a bowl and blend filling into a thick, doughy paste using a hand-held electric mixer or stand mixer fitted with paddle on medium-low speed.

Roll out dough and stamp into rounds as directed on page 12. Place 1 teaspoon filling on each dough round; brush with egg wash, fold, pinch, and seal as directed.

Pour water into a large pot. Whisk in baking soda and brown sugar. Cover and bring to a boil over medium heat. Add pierogies 3 to 4 at a time and poach 15 seconds. Remove with tongs or a metal strainer and transfer to baking sheet. Brush pierogies with oil or leftover egg wash and sprinkle with pretzel or sea salt. Bake until shiny and browned, 10 to 15 minutes. Watch carefully; the filling will ooze out if pierogies overcook.

DO AHEAD: Filling can be made up to 5 days ahead. Cover and refrigerate.

Makes approximately 24 🏛

1 cup (4 ounces, 113 grams) finely shredded Cheddar cheese

2 tablespoons (1 ounce, 28 grams) cream cheese, room temperature

2 tablespoons unbleached all-purpose flour

1/2 teaspoon kosher salt

1/4 teaspoon garlic powder

1 batch Basic Savory Dough (page 16)

8 cups water

1/2 cup baking soda

2 tablespoons packed light or dark brown sugar

Vegetable or canola oil

Pretzel salt or coarse sea salt

SCALLION PANCAKE PIEROGIES
with Asian Dipping Sauce

CRISPY AND CHEWY, the scallion pancake is a perfect subject for pierogi-zation. (Yes, I just invented that word right now.) Keep dough scraps on hand when filling pierogies: Sometimes scallions pop through, so you may have to plug a few holes.

FOR PIEROGIES: Heat oil in a 3^1/2-quart Dutch oven or heavy pot over medium-high heat. Add chicken and cook until browned, about 5 minutes. Flip the chicken and stir in next 4 ingredients. Cook about 5 minutes more. Stir in next 4 ingredients and bring to a simmer. Reduce heat, cover, and simmer until chicken is very tender, 40 to 45 minutes. Uncover; if liquid hasn't fully reduced to a thick and sticky sauce, continue simmering until it does. Shred chicken and sauce with 2 forks, or place into a stand mixer bowl and shred with the paddle on low speed.

Make a batch of dough with the following changes: Reduce butter from 3 tablespoons to 1 tablespoon, and whisk sesame oil in with egg, sour cream, butter, and salt. Once dough is rough and shaggy, knead in scallion.

Roll out dough and stamp into rounds as directed on page 12. Place 1 teaspoon filling on each dough round; brush with egg wash, fold, pinch, and seal as directed.

FOR SAUCE: Whisk first 4 ingredients in a bowl until honey dissolves. Divide among 4 shallow bowls. Sprinkle each with scallion if desired.

Deep-fry, boil, and/or pan-fry pierogies as directed on page 13. Divide evenly among 4 plates and serve with sauce.

DO AHEAD: Filling can be made up to 2 days ahead and sauce without scallions can be made up to 1 week ahead. Cover and refrigerate separately.

Makes approximately 24 🥟

PIEROGIES

2 tablespoons vegetable oil

1 pound skinless, boneless chicken thighs, chopped into 2-inch pieces

1 large shallot, minced

1 large garlic clove, minced

1 half-inch-thick piece fresh ginger, peeled and minced

^{1}/2 teaspoon crushed red pepper flakes

1 cup chicken broth

1 tablespoon soy sauce

1 tablespoon unseasoned rice vinegar

1 tablespoon light brown sugar

1 batch Basic Savory Dough (page 16)

2 tablespoons toasted sesame oil

^{1}/2 cup minced scallions, green parts only

SAUCE

2 tablespoons soy sauce

2 tablespoons unseasoned rice vinegar

2 tablespoons honey

^{1}/2 teaspoon hot chili sesame oil or garlic-chili paste

1 minced scallion, green parts only (optional)

SHORT RIB PIEROGIES
with Beef Gravy

Makes approximately 24

1 tablespoon vegetable or olive oil

2 pounds bone-in beef short ribs

Kosher salt

Freshly ground pepper

2 medium celery stalks, diced

1 small red onion, diced

1 tablespoon tomato paste

2 teaspoons Worcestershire sauce

1 12-ounce bottle stout, porter, or brown ale

1 cup (or more) beef broth or stock

2 tablespoons water

1 tablespoon cornstarch

1 batch Basic Savory Dough, Rye Dough, or Gnocchi Dough (pages 16–18)

I'M NOT ALONE IN BELIEVING PIEROGIES are worthy of more than a family potluck—Michael Symon, a fellow Rust Belt food lover, can't take his signature beef cheek pierogies off the menu at his fancy flagship Cleveland restaurant Lola. Here's my homage to this semi-famous dish that will really stick to your ribs . . . oh, come on, you knew that was coming.

❧❀❦ ♥ ❧❀❦ ♥ ❧❀❦ ♥ ❧❀❦ ♥ ❧❀❦ ♥ ❧❀❦

Preheat oven to 300 degrees. Heat oil in a $3^1/_2$-quart Dutch oven or heavy ovenproof pot over medium-high heat. Generously sprinkle short ribs with salt and pepper. Add short ribs to Dutch oven and brown well on all sides. Transfer ribs to plate. Add celery and onion to Dutch oven and reduce heat to medium-low. Cook until onions are very soft and beginning to caramelize, stirring occasionally, about 15 minutes. Stir in tomato paste and Worcestershire sauce and cook 2 minutes. Add beer and 1 cup broth. Return ribs to Dutch oven. Cook until meat is very tender and falling off the bone, about $1^1/_2$ hours.

Remove ribs from cooking liquid to cool. Strain liquid and discard solids. Cover liquid and refrigerate until fat solidifies and separates from liquid.

When ribs are cool, pull meat off bones and shred, discarding bones, fat, and gristle. Scrape solidified fat off chilled liquid and discard; you should have 1 cup liquid. If not, add enough additional broth to equal 1 cup. Transfer to a small saucepan and bring to a simmer. Whisk water and cornstarch in a bowl. Whisk into simmering liquid and cook until gravy thickens, 2 to 3 minutes.

Place 1 heaping cup (4 ounces, 113 grams) shredded meat and 2 tablespoons gravy in a mini food processor and pulse until coarsely ground. (Reserve remaining meat for another use.)

Roll out dough and stamp into rounds as directed on page 12. Place 1 teaspoon filling on each round; brush with egg wash, fold, pinch, and seal as directed. Deep-fry, boil, and/or pan-fry pierogies as directed on page 13. Serve immediately with remaining gravy.

DO AHEAD: Short ribs can be made up to 5 days ahead and gravy can be made up to 2 days ahead. Cover and refrigerate separately. Bring short ribs to room temperature before using. Reheat gravy before using.

BBQ PULLED PORK PIEROGIES

FULL DISCLOSURE: you only need a small quantity of pulled pork to fill your pierogies, but nature doesn't make small pork shoulders. So I'm giving you my favorite recipe for making an entire tender, juicy, melt-in-your-mouth pork shoulder overnight in the slow cooker. You can freeze any leftover cooked pork shoulder for future use in enchiladas, casseroles, sandwiches, or whatever your heart desires. It might be one of the most valuable recipes in the book!

FOR PIEROGIES: Stir first 8 ingredients in a bowl. Rub spice blend liberally onto pork shoulder. Place onions, carrots, and garlic in bottom of 7-quart slow cooker or large Dutch oven. Set pork atop vegetables. Pour can of tomatoes and beer around pork. Cover and cook on low 8 hours in a slow cooker or in a 325-degree oven for 3 to 4 hours, until fork-tender. Transfer pork to platter until cool enough to handle. Discard vegetables.

Shred cooled pork by hand into bite-size strips, discarding large chunks of fat. Or tear pork into palm-size pieces, discarding any large chunks of fat, place into a stand mixer bowl and shred with the paddle on low speed.

continued >

Makes approximately 24

PIEROGIES

2 tablespoons kosher salt

1 tablespoon freshly ground pepper

1 teaspoon smoked paprika

1 teaspoon garlic powder

$1/2$ teaspoon ground coriander

$1/2$ teaspoon ground fennel seed

$1/4$ teaspoon fresh or dried thyme

$1/4$ teaspoon celery seeds

1 4- to 5-pound bone-in pork shoulder (also called picnic shoulder) or 1 3- to 4- pound boneless pork shoulder

2 medium onions, cut into chunks

4 large carrots, peeled and halved

4 garlic cloves, halved

1 14-ounce can diced tomatoes

1 12-ounce bottle beer of choice

BBQ SAUCE

1 tablespoon vegetable or olive oil

1 small or $^1/_2$ medium red onion, minced

4 garlic cloves, minced

1 cup (12 ounces, 340 grams) ketchup

$^3/_4$ cup (6 fluid ounces) dark beer, such as a brown ale or dark lager

2 tablespoons apple cider vinegar

2 tablespoons honey

1 teaspoon dry mustard powder

1 teaspoon pure chile powder, such as Ancho or California

1 teaspoon kosher salt

1 teaspoon freshly ground pepper

$^1/_2$ teaspoon smoked paprika

1 batch Basic Savory Dough (page 16)

FOR SAUCE: Heat oil in a medium saucepan over medium heat. Add onion and garlic and cook until onion is soft and starting to caramelize, stirring frequently, about 10 minutes. Whisk in next 9 ingredients and bring to a simmer. Cook until sauce has reduced and thickened, about 40 minutes.

Place 1 heaping cup (4 ounces, 113 grams) shredded pork and $^1/_4$ cup sauce in a mini food processor and pulse until coarsely ground. (Reserve remaining pork for another meal, and reserve remaining sauce for dipping or for another use.)

Roll out dough and stamp into rounds as directed on page 12. Place 1 teaspoon filling on each round; brush with egg wash, fold, pinch, and seal as directed. Deep-fry, boil, and/or pan-fry pierogies as directed on page 13. Serve immediately with remaining sauce if desired.

DO AHEAD: Pork can be made up to 5 days ahead; wrap and freeze if making more than 24 hours ahead or cover and refrigerate if making 1 day ahead. Sauce can be made up to 1 week ahead. Cover and refrigerate.

FRENCH ONION SOUP DUMPLING PIEROGIES

ADMITTEDLY, this is a crazy globe-trotting culinary mash-up: Provence by way of Krakow by way of Shanghai. But somehow the combination of France's most comforting soup and China's most jaw-dropping dumpling works when you put them both in pierogi form. Try not to be weirded out by making what amounts to beef Jell-O: it's the key to getting that soupy liquid into the dumpling. Don't be tempted to deep-fry or pan-fry these pierogies—stick to boiling them to keep the filling from leaking out.

≫❀≪ ♥ ≫❀≪ ♥ ≫❀≪ ♥ ≫❀≪ ♥ ≫❀≪ ♥ ≫❀≪

FOR PIEROGIES: Melt butter in a medium saucepan over medium-low heat. Add onion, salt, and pepper and cook until onion is very soft and brown, stirring occasionally, about 30 minutes. Stir in wine, scraping up browned bits, and cook until wine is mostly absorbed, 3 to 5 minutes. Stir in broth and bring to a simmer. Cook for about 30 minutes to allow the flavors to meld.

Pour water into a small bowl. Sprinkle gelatin over and let sit for 5 minutes. Whisk hydrated gelatin into onion soup and cook until gelatin dissolves, about 1 minute. Pour into bowl and refrigerate uncovered until firm, about 2 hours.

Roll out dough and stamp into rounds as directed on page 12. Place 1 teaspoon filling on each dough round; brush with egg wash, fold, pinch, and seal as directed.

continued >

Makes approximately 24 🥟

PIEROGIES

1 tablespoon unsalted butter

3/4 pound yellow onion (about 1 large), halved lengthwise and thinly sliced into strips along the "grain"

1/2 teaspoon kosher salt

1/4 teaspoon freshly ground pepper

1/4 cup dry white wine

1 1/2 cups beef broth

2 tablespoons water

1 envelope (1 tablespoon) powdered gelatin

1 batch Basic Savory Dough (page 16)

FRICO

1¹/₂ cups (6 ounces, 170 grams) finely shredded Gruyere cheese

FOR FRICO: Preheat broiler. Line a baking sheet with parchment paper or a silicone liner. Mound about 1 tablespoon cheese for each frico 2 inches apart on baking sheet. Repeat until all cheese is used; depending on baking sheet size, you may need to broil in 2 batches to make 24 fricos. Broil until cheese melts completely. Let fricos rest on baking sheet until cool and crisp.

Boil pierogies, 1 to 2 minutes for fresh and 3 to 4 minutes for frozen. Top each pierogi with a frico and serve immediately.

DO AHEAD: Filling can be made up to 5 days ahead. Cover and refrigerate.

CORN CHOWDER PIEROGIES

Makes approximately 24

1 small to medium ear fresh corn

2 cups whole or reduced-fat milk

1 large garlic clove, halved

1/2 pound (8 ounces, 227 grams) Yukon Gold potatoes, peeled and chopped into 2-inch pieces (about 1 medium or 2 small)

1 tablespoon minced red bell pepper

1 tablespoon minced celery

1/2 teaspoon kosher salt

1 batch Basic Savory Dough or Gnocchi Dough (pages 16–18)

PEOPLE THINK OF CHOWDER as a hearty cold-weather food, but in July and August, when corn is at its sweetest, I can't stop sucking down bowls of fresh corn chowder like it's my job. (Hey, it kind of is my job.) Steeping the cobs in milk infuses extra corn flavor into every ingredient in this recipe—believe me, you'll be using almost every drop of it, so it's well worth the time.

Using a sharp knife, slice corn kernels off the cob into a bowl and set aside. Break the cob into 2 or 3 pieces and place in a medium saucepan. Add milk and garlic. Bring to a boil over medium heat; do not let boil over. Remove from heat. Cover and let stand at room temperature at least 1 hour and up to 3 hours.

Remove cobs and garlic from milk and discard. Place potatoes in same milk and return to a boil over medium heat. Reduce heat and simmer until potatoes are tender, about 15 minutes. Transfer potatoes to a bowl. Reserve milk in pan. Add reserved corn kernels, red pepper, and celery to milk and return to a simmer; cook until vegetables are tender, 3 to 5 minutes. Run potatoes through a ricer or food mill fitted with fine disk into bowl, or mash in bowl with a potato masher until no lumps remain. Stir in salt and just enough reserved milk to make potatoes smooth, about 1 tablespoon. Remove vegetables from milk and stir into potatoes. Discard milk (finally!). Refrigerate until cool and firm, about 1 hour.

Roll out dough and stamp into rounds as directed on page 12. Place 1 teaspoon filling on each dough round; brush with egg wash, fold, pinch, and seal as directed. Deep-fry, boil, and/or pan-fry pierogies as directed on page 13.

DO AHEAD: Milk can be steeped and strained up to 2 days ahead. Potato filling can be made up to 1 day ahead. Cover and refrigerate.

SWEET PIEROGIES

SOUR CHERRY PIEROGIES

THE TRADITIONAL UKRAINIAN WAY to make these pierogies is to place a few tiny pitted fresh sour cherries in the middle of each dough round, sprinkle with sugar, and seal. I'm switching things up just a bit to let pectin gel all that gorgeous cherry juice

If using fresh cherries, toss with $1/2$ cup sugar in a bowl and let sit until cherries release juice, stirring occasionally, about 30 minutes. Strain juice into a bowl; you should have about 1 cup. If using jarred cherries in juice, strain juice into a bowl, reserving 1 cup. Stir $1/2$ cup sugar into juice until dissolved.

Coarsely chop cherries and place in a medium saucepan. Whisk remaining $1/4$ cup sugar and pectin in a bowl, then stir into cherries. Bring to a simmer over medium-low heat. Cook just until liquid becomes thick and syrupy, stirring occasionally, 10 to 15 minutes. Transfer to a bowl and refrigerate at least 1 hour.

MAKE CHERRY SYRUP: Bring reserved cherry juice and maple syrup to a simmer in a small saucepan over medium-low heat. Cook until liquid has reduced by a third to a half, about 10 minutes. The syrup will be bubbly and loose, but thickens as it cools.

Roll out dough and stamp into rounds as directed on page 12. Place 1 teaspoon filling on each dough round; brush with egg wash, fold, pinch, and seal as directed. Deep-fry, boil, and/or pan-fry pierogies as directed on page 13. Serve immediately with cherry syrup and creme fraiche if desired.

DO AHEAD: Filling and syrup can be made up to 1 week ahead. Cover and refrigerate separately.

Makes approximately 24

1 pound pitted fresh sour cherries or 1 24-ounce jar sour cherries

$1/2$ cup ($3^{1}/_{2}$ ounces, 100 grams) plus $1/4$ cup ($1^{3}/_{4}$ ounces, 50 grams) sugar

2 teaspoons powdered low-sugar pectin

2 tablespoons maple syrup

1 batch Basic Sweet Dough (page 16)

Creme fraiche for serving (optional)

RICE PUDDING PIEROGIES
with Cranberry Compote

Makes approximately 24

PIEROGIES

2 cups whole milk

1/4 teaspoon ground cinnamon

1/4 teaspoon ground ginger

1/2 cup (3 1/2 ounces, 100 grams) Arborio rice

1/4 cup (1 3/4 ounces, 50 grams) sugar

1 batch Oat Dough (page 17)

COMPOTE

2 cups (7 ounces, 198 grams) fresh or thawed frozen cranberries

1/4 cup (1 3/4 ounces, 50 grams) sugar

1 cinnamon stick

1/2 whole star anise pod

1 tablespoon vanilla extract

RICE PUDDING'S something you either love to pieces or hate with a fiery passion. Judging by this recipe, I'm sure you can guess on which side of the argument I fall. Arborio rice, the grain usually used for chewy-creamy risotto, adds a lovely bit of texture to this filling. And even if rice pudding isn't your thing, I hope you'll try out the cranberry compote—it's a tart counterpoint that would be equally tasty on top of tapioca pudding or oatmeal.

FOR PIEROGIES: Bring milk to a simmer in a small saucepan over medium-low heat. Whisk in cinnamon and ginger. Stir in rice and cook until rice is tender and milk is almost completely absorbed, stirring frequently, 25 to 30 minutes. Stir in sugar until dissolved. Transfer to a bowl and refrigerate at least 1 hour.

Roll out dough and stamp into rounds as directed on page 12. Place 1 teaspoon filling on each dough round; brush with egg wash, fold, pinch, and seal as directed. Deep-fry, boil, and/or pan-fry pierogies as directed on page 13.

FOR COMPOTE: Stir cranberries, sugar, cinnamon, and star anise in a bowl. Let stand 30 minutes, stirring occasionally, to begin dissolving sugar and softening cranberries.

Transfer to a small saucepan and add vanilla. Cook over medium-low heat, stirring frequently, until sugar dissolves into liquid and comes to a simmer. Cook a few minutes more until cranberries soften but still remain whole.

Serve pierogies with compote.

DO AHEAD: Filling can be made up to 3 days ahead and compote can be made up to 1 week ahead. Cover and refrigerate separately. Reheat compote before serving.

LEMON-RICOTTA PIEROGIES
with Honeyed Brown Butter

THIS DUMPLING OWES an equal debt to Italian cheesecake, a dense and slightly crumbly cake made with ricotta and fragrant with citrus zest, as well as my favorite lazy-day breakfast of lemon-ricotta pancakes. Served with honeyed brown butter, these could easily make their way into the regular brunch rotation. The lemon extract here is a lovely enhancement to the zest; I know it's kind of annoying to buy small bottles of extract and have them rattling around your pantry, but I love what it does to the flavor.

FOR PIEROGIES: Stir ricotta, zest of 1 lemon, sugar, nutmeg, and $^1/_2$ teaspoon lemon extract in a bowl.

Make a batch of dough with the following changes: Whisk remaining lemon zest and remaining $^1/_2$ teaspoon lemon extract in with egg, sour cream, butter, sugar and salt in dough recipe. Roll out dough and stamp into rounds as directed on page 12. Place 1 teaspoon filling on each dough round; brush with egg wash, fold, pinch, and seal as directed. Deep-fry, boil, and/or pan-fry pierogies as directed on page 13.

FOR BUTTER: Melt butter in a small saucepan over medium-low heat and cook until butter separates. The white solid bits initially rising to the top of the liquid will fall to the bottom of the pan and start to brown as the butter turns deep gold and begins to smell gorgeously nutty. Immediately remove from heat; do not let butter burn. Whisk in honey and lemon.

Serve pierogies with brown butter.

DO AHEAD: Filling can be made up to 2 days ahead. Cover and refrigerate. Butter is best made fresh, but can be made 1 day ahead. Cover and refrigerate, and reheat over low heat before serving.

Makes approximately 24 🥟

PIEROGIES

$^3/_4$ cup (6 ounces, 170 grams) fresh ricotta cheese

Zest of 2 medium to large lemons, separated

2 tablespoons powdered sugar

$^1/_4$ teaspoon freshly grated nutmeg

1 teaspoon lemon extract, divided into $^1/_2$ teaspoons (optional)

1 batch Basic Sweet Dough (page 16)

BUTTER

4 tablespoons (2 ounces, 57 grams) unsalted butter

2 tablespoons honey

1 tablespoon freshly squeezed lemon juice

FIG, GOAT CHEESE, AND BLACK PEPPER PIEROGIES

THE MINUTE YOU SEE FRESH FIGS at the market, scoop up those sweet and juicy stunners for this irresistibly sophisticated pierogi recipe. (Know someone with a fig tree in the backyard? You're even luckier and I'm officially seething with jealousy.) For a sweet-and-savory pairing of goat cheese goodness, serve these at a cocktail party with the mushroom, goat cheese, and chive pierogies on page <OV>.

≫✿≪ ♥ ≫✿≪ ♥ ≫✿≪ ♥ ≫✿≪ ♥ ≫✿≪ ♥ ≫✿≪

Preheat oven to 300 degrees. Line a baking sheet with parchment paper or a silicone liner. Place figs cut-side up on baking sheet. Bake until figs are soft and slightly oozing with juice, about 45 minutes.

Transfer figs to a cutting board until cool enough to handle. Chop into rough $1/2$-inch pieces. Transfer to a bowl. Stir in goat cheese, sugar, and $1/2$ teaspoon pepper.

Make a batch of dough, whisking remaining 1 teaspoon pepper in with the flour. Roll dough out and stamp into rounds as directed on page 12. Place 1 teaspoon filling on each dough round; brush with egg wash, fold, pinch, and seal as directed. Deep-fry, boil, and/or pan-fry pierogies as directed on page 13.

DO AHEAD: Filling can be made up to 3 days ahead. Cover and refrigerate.

Makes approximately 24 🏛

8 fresh black Mission figs, halved

$1/3$ cup (3 ounces, 85 grams) goat cheese, room temperature

$1 1/2$ teaspoons demerara or turbinado sugar

$1/2$ teaspoon plus 1 teaspoon freshly ground pepper

1 batch Basic Sweet Dough (page 16)

NUTELLA PIEROGIES
with Bananas Foster Sauce

Makes approximately 24

PIEROGIES

1 cup (5 ounces, 142 grams) whole hazelnuts

¹/₄ cup (1³/₄ ounces, 50 grams) sugar

2 tablespoons unsweetened cocoa powder

1 tablespoon oat flour or unbleached all-purpose flour

1 batch Cocoa Dough (page 17)

Powdered sugar for serving (optional)

ONCE YOU'VE MADE HOMEMADE NUTELLA, I'm not sure you can ever go back to buying the oily processed jarred version again. This filling is slightly thicker and more granular than what you'd want to spread on toast so it keeps its integrity when heated inside the pierogi. For a spreadable breakfast version, omit the flour and add 1 tablespoon vegetable oil or nut oil to the food processor, and grind to your preferred consistency. For a nonalcoholic Bananas Foster sauce, skip the rum, but remember, the sauce won't flambé without it.

FOR PIEROGIES: Skin the hazelnuts: Preheat oven to 350 degrees. Scatter hazelnuts in a single layer on a rimmed baking sheet. Toast nuts until skins starts to crack and separate, 10 to 15 minutes. Pour hazelnuts onto a clean kitchen towel, loosely fold closed, and rub to flake off skins. Unfold towel and remove skinned hazelnuts; use caution as nuts might still be hot. Repeat with any stubborn unskinned nuts and don't worry if some bits of skin remain.

Pour skinned hazelnuts into food processor and grind until reduced to a fine powder. Scrape down sides of the bowl, then add sugar, cocoa powder, and flour. Grind until granular paste forms; filling should be almost Play-Doh-like in consistency.

Roll out dough and stamp into rounds as directed on page 12. Place 1 teaspoon filling on each round; brush with egg wash, fold, pinch, and seal as directed. Deep-fry, boil, and/or pan-fry pierogies as directed on page 13.

continued >

BANANAS FOSTER SAUCE

2 tablespoons (1 ounce, 28 grams) unsalted butter

$1/4$ cup ($1^7/8$ ounces, 53 grams) packed dark brown sugar

$1/4$ teaspoon ground allspice or cinnamon

1 small pinch kosher salt

2 ripe bananas, sliced $1/2$-inch thick

2 tablespoons dark or spiced rum

FOR SAUCE: Melt butter in a medium skillet over medium heat. Add sugar, allspice, and salt, and cook until the sugar dissolves and starts to bubble, stirring frequently, 3 to 5 minutes. Stir in banana slices and cook until softened and warmed through, 2 to 3 minutes. Remove skillet from heat and add rum. Return skillet to heat, carefully and quickly flambéing sauce with long barbecue lighter or long match. Cook until flames die down.

Serve pierogies with warm sauce, dusting with powdered sugar if desired.

DO AHEAD: Nutella can be made up to 1 week ahead and sauce can be made up to 2 days ahead, though it can't be flambéed if made ahead. Cover and refrigerate separately. Reheat sauce before serving.

FRIED APPLE PIE-ROGIES
with Peanut Butter Caramel

IF YOU'RE A JUNK FOOD LOVER of a certain age and you grew up eating the real McDonald's apple pies—the ones that were truly fried, not baked, and so molten inside that they were most definitely a burn lawsuit waiting to happen—then these pierogies will be a piping-hot blast from the past. The peanut butter caramel on the side is just gilding the lily.

FOR PIEROGIES: Melt butter in a small saucepan over medium-low heat. Stir in apples, cover, and cook until apples begin to soften, about 5 minutes. Uncover and stir in sugar, vanilla bean paste, and cinnamon and cook, stirring occasionally, until apples are very soft and liquid is mostly absorbed, about 10 minutes. Transfer to a bowl and refrigerate at least 1 hour.

Roll out dough and stamp into rounds as directed on page 12. Place 1 teaspoon filling on each dough round; brush with egg wash, fold, pinch, and seal as directed.

If deep-frying pierogies, whisk egg and water in shallow bowl. Place graham cracker crumbs in another shallow bowl. Dip each fresh or frozen pierogi in egg wash, allowing excess to drip back into bowl, then dredge in crumbs, shaking off excess. Place on a baking sheet and deep-fry as directed on page 13.

If boiling then pan-frying pierogies, boil until softened, about 2 minutes for fresh or 3 to 4 minutes for frozen. Transfer to a baking sheet until cool enough to handle. Dip and coat pierogies as directed above and pan-fry as directed on page 13.

continued >

Makes approximately 24 🥟

PIEROGIES

1 tablespoon unsalted butter

$^1/_2$ pound (8 ounces, 227 grams) crisp apple (about 1 medium), peeled, cored, and cut into $^1/_4$-inch cubes

2 tablespoons packed light brown sugar

$^1/_2$ teaspoon vanilla bean paste

$^1/_4$ teaspoon ground cinnamon

1 batch Oat Dough or Basic Sweet Dough (pages 16–17)

1 egg

1 tablespoon water

1 cup finely ground graham cracker crumbs (about 1 sleeve of graham crackers)

FOR CARAMEL: Stir sugar, water, and corn syrup in a medium high-sided saucepan over medium heat until sugar dissolves. Let sugar syrup come to a boil without stirring, swirling pan periodically if desired. Continue boiling as syrup deepens in color and starts to smell caramelized. As soon as syrup is a rich whiskey color, remove pan from heat. Immediately whisk in cream in a slow, steady stream; be careful as caramel will bubble and may splatter. (If it seizes and hardens, return pan to low heat and keep whisking until caramel re-melts.) Off heat, whisk in peanut butter. Let cool at least 15 minutes.

Serve pierogies with caramel sauce.

DO AHEAD: Filling can be made up to 3 days ahead and caramel can be made up to 1 week ahead. Cover and refrigerate separately.

CARAMEL

$1/2$ cup ($3^1/2$ ounces, 100 grams) sugar

2 tablespoons water

1 teaspoon light corn syrup or Lyle's Golden Syrup

$1/4$ cup heavy cream

2 tablespoons creamy peanut butter (do not use natural)

PEANUT BUTTER AND JELLY PIEROGIES

Makes approximately 24 🏛

1 cup (5 ounces, 142 grams) roasted unsalted peanuts

2 tablespoons powdered sugar

1/8 teaspoon kosher salt

1 teaspoon light corn syrup or Lyle's Golden Syrup

1/2 cup fruit jam (or pick any fruit filling from this book)

1 batch Basic Sweet Dough, Oat Dough, or Whole-Wheat Dough (pages 16–17)

MAKE SURE YOU USE the freshest peanuts you can get your paws on when making your homemade peanut butter—the flavor comes through loud and clear, so if your nuts are stale or rancid, believe me, you'll know. Don't want to make your own peanut butter? (Uh, why not? It's awesome!) You can use fresh-ground from the machine at the grocery store, but sweeten it up with powdered sugar until it's no longer liquid and holds its shape.

＞＞❂≪ ❤ ＞＞❂≪ ❤ ＞＞❂≪ ❤ ＞＞❂≪ ❤ ＞＞❂≪ ❤ ＞＞❂≪

Grind peanuts, sugar, and salt to a coarse paste in a mini food processor. Add corn syrup and grind until peanut butter forms.

Roll out dough and stamp into rounds as directed on page 12. Place 1/2 teaspoon jam on each dough round, then top with 1/2 teaspoon peanut butter filling. Brush with egg wash, fold, pinch, and seal as directed. Deep-fry, boil, and/or pan-fry pierogies as directed on page 13.

DO AHEAD: Peanut butter can be made up to 1 week ahead. Cover and refrigerate.

PEANUT BUTTER-CHOCOLATE PIEROGIES

I HAVE AN EMBARRASSING confession to make: when I was a kid, for some crazy reason I decided I didn't like Reese's peanut butter cups and shunned them like they were lima beans. So every Halloween when I dumped my trick-or-treat haul onto the living room floor, I carefully picked every peanut butter cup out of my stash and gave them to my dad. GAVE THEM AWAY! How could I have been so blind? Thankfully, now I see the error of my ways and no one lays a finger on my Reese's stash. Or my peanut butter-chocolate pierogies.

❧ ❦ ❧ ❥ ❧ ❦ ❧ ❥ ❧ ❦ ❧ ❥ ❧ ❦ ❧ ❥ ❧ ❦ ❧ ❥ ❧ ❦ ❧

Place chocolate in a heatproof (stainless steel or Pyrex) bowl. Whisk cream and sugar in a very small saucepan over medium-low heat just until cream comes to a simmer. Pour over chocolate and let sit for 1 minute, then whisk gently until chocolate melts completely. Refrigerate until completely firm.

Grind peanuts, sugar, and salt to a coarse paste in a mini food processor. Add corn syrup and grind until peanut butter forms.

Roll out dough and stamp into rounds as directed on page 12. Place 1/2 teaspoon peanut butter filling on each dough round, then top with 1/2 teaspoon chocolate filling. Brush with egg wash, fold, pinch, and seal as directed. Deep-fry, boil, and/or pan-fry pierogies as directed on page 13.

DO AHEAD: Both fillings can be made up to 1 week ahead. Cover and refrigerate separately.

Makes approximately 24

1/3 cup (2 ounces, 57 grams) bittersweet or semisweet chocolate, chopped into small chunks

1/4 cup heavy cream

1 tablespoon sugar

1 cup (5 ounces, 142 grams) roasted unsalted peanuts

2 tablespoons powdered sugar

1/8 teaspoon kosher salt

1 teaspoon light corn syrup or Lyle's Golden Syrup

1 batch Cocoa Dough (page 17)

SWEET FARMER'S CHEESE PIEROGIES

Makes approximately 24

1/2 pound (8 ounces, 227 grams) farmer's cheese

2 tablespoons sugar

1 tablespoon honey

1 teaspoon vanilla bean paste

1 batch Basic Sweet Dough (page 16)

FARMER'S CHEESE, a soft and crumbly fresh cheese, is one of the traditional Eastern European fillings for both sweet and savory pierogies. If you can't find it in your local market's dairy case, you can substitute fresh ricotta—just drain the ricotta for a few hours through a large coffee filter or flour sack towel to remove excess moisture. Want a fancy accompaniment? Make a batch of Honeyed Brown Butter (page 81) or Bourbon Maple Butter (facing).

Stir cheese, sugar, honey, and vanilla bean paste in a bowl.

Roll out dough and stamp into rounds as directed on page 12. Place 1 teaspoon filling on each dough round; brush with egg wash, fold, pinch, and seal as directed. Deep-fry, boil, and/or pan-fry pierogies as directed on page 13. Serve immediately.

DO AHEAD: Filling can be made up to 3 days ahead. Cover and refrigerate.

PUMPKIN PIEROGIES
with Bourbon Maple Butter

I'LL NEVER BE THE PERSON who steals the last piece of pumpkin pie at the holiday dessert table—something about the way it wiggles and wobbles freaks me out. But watch out when these pumpkin pierogies are around, because I can't stop stuffing these seasonal sweeties in my pie hole! They're filled with a sweet but simple pumpkin butter, with none of that strangely smooth flan-like ookiness.

FOR PIEROGIES: Stir pumpkin, sugar, allspice, and cinnamon in a small saucepan over medium-low heat. Cook down into pumpkin butter, stirring frequently, about 45 minutes. Filling will be very thick and easy to scrape off the bottom of the pan without residue. Transfer to a bowl and refrigerate at least 1 hour.

Roll out dough and stamp into rounds as directed on page 12. Place 1 teaspoon filling on each dough round; brush with egg wash, fold, pinch, and seal as directed. Deep-fry, boil, and/or pan-fry pierogies as directed on page 13.

FOR BUTTER: Melt butter in a small saucepan over medium-low heat. Whisk in syrup, bourbon, and vanilla bean paste.

Serve pierogies with warm butter, either for drizzling or dipping.

DO AHEAD: Filling and sauce can be made up to 1 week ahead. Cover and refrigerate separately. Reheat sauce before serving.

Makes approximately 24

PIEROGIES

1 15-ounce can pure pumpkin puree (not pumpkin pie filling)

1/4 cup (1 7/8 ounces, 53 grams) packed dark brown sugar

1/4 teaspoon ground allspice

1/4 teaspoon ground cinnamon

1 batch Basic Sweet Dough, Whole-Wheat Dough, or Oat Dough (pages 16–17)

BUTTER

8 tablespoons (4 ounces, 113 grams) unsalted butter

1/4 cup dark maple syrup

2 tablespoons bourbon

1/2 teaspoon vanilla bean paste

ELVIS (PEANUT BUTTER, BANANA, AND BACON) PIEROGIES

Makes approximately 24

1/2 cup (4 3/4 ounces, 135 grams) creamy or chunky peanut butter

2 heaping tablespoons coarsely chopped banana (about 1 small banana)

2 heaping tablespoons finely chopped cooked bacon (about 2 slices bacon)

2 tablespoons (1 ounce, 28 grams) powdered sugar

1 batch Basic Sweet Dough (page 16)

Powdered sugar or Bananas Foster Sauce (page 86)

"A LITTLE LESS CONVERSATION, a little more action!" your loved ones will shout once you start to make these little hunka hunka burning loves. Suspicious minds might wonder why they're disappearing from the plate so quickly, but how could you not love them tender when they're stuffed with that classic combo of peanut butter, banana, and bacon? (BTW, the King would really want you to deep-fry these.)

❧❀❧ ♥ ❧❀❧ ♥ ❧❀❧ ♥ ❧❀❧ ♥ ❧❀❧ ♥ ❧❀❧

Stir peanut butter, banana, bacon, and sugar in a bowl until blended.

Roll out dough and stamp into rounds as directed on page 12. Place 1 teaspoon filling on each dough round; brush with egg wash, fold, pinch, and seal as directed. Deep-fry, boil, and/or pan-fry pierogies as directed on page 13.

Serve pierogies sprinkled with powdered sugar or with warm Bananas Foster Sauce. Or both!

DO AHEAD: The filling can be made up to 2 days ahead. Cover and refrigerate.

MOUNDS BAR AND ALMOND JOY PIEROGIES

Makes approximately 24 🥟

1 large egg white

1/4 cup (1 3/4 ounces, 50 grams) sugar

1/4 teaspoon cream of tartar

1 cup (3 ounces, 85 grams) shredded sweetened coconut

1 batch Cocoa Dough (page 17)

24 roasted unsalted almonds (optional)

Semisweet Chocolate Sauce (page 107, optional)

WE DON'T GET A LOT OF TRICK-OR-TREATERS at our house—and by "don't get a lot," I mean we maybe get two or three kids ringing our doorbell each year. But why would this stop me from buying a bag of Halloween candy? Not that anyone who has the temerity to show up at our door would ever get a Mounds or Almond Joy out of that bag—I've already extracted them and saved them for myself.

❧ ❀ ❦ ♥ ❧ ❀ ❦ ♥ ❧ ❀ ❦ ♥ ❧ ❀ ❦ ♥ ❧ ❀ ❦ ♥ ❧ ❀ ❦

Fill a small saucepan halfway with water and bring to a simmer over medium heat. Whisk egg white and sugar in a heatproof (stainless steel or Pyrex) bowl. Set bowl atop pan of simmering water; do not let bowl touch water. Whisk constantly until sugar dissolves and liquid is frothy and warm to touch, 2 to 3 minutes. Remove bowl from heat. Using hand-held electric mixer on medium-high speed, beat white until thick and glossy, 1 to 2 minutes. Add cream of tartar and continue beating until stiff peaks form, 1 to 2 minutes. Stir in coconut. Let sit until coconut absorbs some of marshmallow and softens, about 1 hour.

Roll out dough and stamp into rounds as directed on page 12. For Mounds pierogies, place 1 teaspoon filling on each dough round; brush with egg wash, fold, pinch, and seal as directed. For Almond Joy pierogies, place 1 teaspoon filling on each dough round, then top with almond; brush with egg wash, fold, pinch, and seal. Deep-fry, boil, and/or pan-fry pierogies as directed on page 13.

Serve pierogies with warm Semisweet Chocolate Sauce if desired.

DO AHEAD: Filling can be made up to 1 day ahead. Cover and refrigerate. Bring to room temperature before using.

PECAN PIE-ROGIES

WOULD YOU BELIEVE THIS YANKEE GAL had never made a pecan pie in her life before she decided to take on this pierogi filling? I don't know what the heck I was waiting for—after whipping this up, I might even dispense with the crust entirely from now on and just eat pecan filling straight from the pan. Let's make it a new holiday tradition.

⟫✿⟪ ♥ ⟫✿⟪ ♥ ⟫✿⟪ ♥ ⟫✿⟪ ♥ ⟫✿⟪ ♥ ⟫✿⟪

Preheat oven to 375 degrees. Scatter pecans in a single layer on a rimmed baking sheet. Bake until nuts are just fragrant, 7 to 8 minutes. Let cool while making filling. Stir egg, corn syrup, butter, and vanilla bean paste in a bowl until well blended. Stir in sugar, flour, and salt. Finely chop toasted pecans and stir into filling. Pour filling into a standard loaf pan or small casserole dish and bake until thickened and set, stirring frequently, about 15 minutes. Scrape into a bowl and cool to room temperature.

Roll out dough and stamp into rounds as directed on page 12. Place 1 teaspoon filling on each round; brush with egg wash, fold, pinch, and seal as directed. Deep-fry, boil and/or pan-fry pierogies as directed on page 13.

DO AHEAD: Filling can be made up to 5 days ahead. Cover and refrigerate. Bring to room temperature before using.

Makes approximately 24 🥟

3/4 cup (3 ounces, 85 grams) pecan halves

1 large egg

1/4 cup (2 3/4 ounces, 78 grams) dark corn syrup

1 tablespoon unsalted butter, melted

1/2 teaspoon vanilla bean paste

1/4 cup (1 7/8 ounces, 53 grams) packed dark brown sugar

1/2 teaspoon unbleached all-purpose flour

1 pinch kosher salt

1 batch Basic Sweet Dough or Oat Dough (pages 16–17)

PINEAPPLE~COCONUT PIEROGIES
with Boozy Tropical Fruit Salad

DESPITE MY REPUTATION as a beer-drinkin', dive bar-hangin' kind of girl, deep within my heart lies a passionate, colorful, exuberant love for tiki culture. (Maybe I spent too much time in Disney World's Enchanted Tiki Room as a kid?) I've already pledged my troth to crab Rangoon (page 37), and now here's my homage to the classic piña colada. I like to spear these pierogies on colorful cocktail toothpicks for a true tiki feel.

FOR PIEROGIES: Bring pineapple and coconut milk to a simmer in a small saucepan over medium heat and cook until coconut milk has reduced by half and pineapple is very soft, 12 to 15 minutes.

Mash pineapple coarsely in saucepan using potato masher or fork. Transfer 2 tablespoons coconut milk from pan into small bowl. Add cornstarch to bowl and whisk until dissolved. Stir sugar into pineapple and continue to cook until liquid is almost completely absorbed, stirring occasionally, 10 to 15 minutes. Stir in cornstarch slurry and cook 30 seconds. Transfer to bowl and cool to room temperature. Stir coconut into filling.

Roll out dough and stamp into rounds as directed on page 12. Place 1 teaspoon filling on each dough round; brush with egg wash, fold, pinch, and seal as directed. Deep-fry, boil, and/or pan-fry pierogies as directed on page 13.

FOR FRUIT SALAD: Stir fruit, rum, and sugar in bowl until sugar dissolves. Let stand at least 2 hours, stirring occasionally.

Serve pierogies with fruit salad.

DO AHEAD: Filling can be made up to 2 days ahead and fruit salad can be made 1 day ahead. Cover and refrigerate separately.

Makes approximately 24

PIEROGIES

1 20-ounce can pineapple chunks, drained

$1/2$ cup light coconut milk

1 teaspoon cornstarch

2 tablespoons sugar

3 tablespoons sweetened flaked coconut

1 batch Basic Sweet Dough (page 16)

FRUIT SALAD

1 large ripe mango (about $1/2$ pound), peeled and diced

2 ripe kiwis, peeled and diced

$1/2$ cup halved maraschino cherries

2 tablespoons spiced rum

1 tablespoon coconut sugar or packed light brown sugar

LEMON CURD PIEROGIES

MAKING LEMON CURD is an impossible exercise in patience for me. Though I know beyond a shadow of a doubt that it tastes best when chilled, I absolutely cannot stop myself from sneaking warm spoonfuls fresh from the bowl. (I have the same problem with homemade tapioca pudding.) But the overnight chill process is crucial here to get the curd to the right consistency. Make the curd 1 day before assembling your pierogies, and work quickly when filling them so the curd stays cool and thick. If you see it start to warm and soften, put the curd back in the fridge for 15 minutes or so, then carry on.

≫❀≪ ♥ ≫❀≪ ♥ ≫❀≪ ♥ ≫❀≪ ♥ ≫❀≪ ♥ ≫❀≪

Whisk cornstarch and water in a bowl. Fill a small saucepan halfway with water and bring to a simmer over medium heat. Whisk lemon juice, sugar, eggs, and zest in a heatproof (stainless steel or Pyrex) bowl. Set bowl atop pan of simmering water; do not let bowl touch water. Whisk until liquid turns from sloshy and translucent to opaque, 3 to 4 minutes. Whisk in cornstarch slurry and continue to cook until liquid thickens into a silken curd consistency, whisking constantly, 1 to 2 minutes—do not let the curd come to a simmer or the eggs will scramble. Remove bowl from heat. Add butter and whisk until completely incorporated. Strain curd through a fine-mesh strainer into a bowl and refrigerate overnight.

Roll out dough and stamp into rounds as directed on page 12. Place 1 teaspoon filling on each dough round; brush with egg wash, fold, pinch, and seal as directed. Deep-fry, boil, and/or pan-fry pierogies as directed on page 13.

DO AHEAD: Filling can be made up to 3 days ahead. Cover and refrigerate.

Makes approximately 24 🥟

1 teaspoon cornstarch

1 tablespoon water

1/3 cup fresh lemon juice (from about 2 small to medium lemons)

1/2 cup (3 1/2 ounces, 100 grams) sugar

2 large eggs

Zest of 1 lemon

1 tablespoon unsalted butter, cut into 4 small cubes

1 batch Basic Sweet Dough (page 16)

CARAMELLO PIEROGIES

Makes approximately 24

Nonstick baking spray

4 tablespoons (2 ounces, 57 grams) unsalted butter

1/2 cup heavy cream, divided in half

1/2 cup (5 1/2 ounces, 156 grams) light corn syrup

1/4 cup (1 3/4 ounces, 50 grams) sugar

1/4 cup (1 7/8 ounces, 53 grams) packed dark brown sugar

1/4 teaspoon kosher salt

1 batch Cocoa Dough (page 17)

Semisweet Chocolate Sauce (page 107, optional)

"EXTRA CARAMEL" is an oxymoron. Think of the leftover caramel you'll have from this recipe as "bonus caramels" to snack on or gift to others. And don't be intimidated by the use of a candy thermometer here: while confectionery pros can judge by sight, it helps us mortals know when the sugar is caramelized but not burnt. Because "ruined caramel" isn't an oxymoron, it's a national tragedy.

Spritz a standard loaf pan with nonstick baking spray. Melt butter in a small high-sided saucepan over medium heat. Stir in 1/4 cup cream, corn syrup, both sugars, and salt and cook, stirring frequently, until sugar dissolves completely and mixture comes to a boil. Clip a candy thermometer to the pan and cook without stirring until thermometer reaches 240 degrees. Remove pan from heat. Stir in remaining 1/4 cup cream; be careful and stand back as caramel will bubble and may splatter. Return pan to heat and cook until thermometer registers 245 degrees. Pour caramel into loaf pan. Let caramel stand at room temperature for 3 hours until hardened enough to cut.

Peel caramel out of pan and place on a cutting board. Cut caramel into 1/2-inch squares using pizza cutter or knife. Reserve 24 squares for pierogies; wrap remaining caramels individually in waxed paper and store at room temperature.

Roll out dough and stamp into rounds as directed on page 12. Place 1 caramel square on each dough round; brush with egg wash, fold, pinch, and seal as directed. Deep-fry, boil, and/or pan-fry pierogies as directed on page 13. Serve immediately with warm semisweet chocolate sauce if desired.

DO AHEAD: Filling can be made up to 2 days ahead. Wrap tightly in waxed paper and store at room temperature.

S'MORES PIEROGIES

Makes approximately 24 🥟

1/4 cup heavy cream

1 tablespoon plus 1/2 cup (3 1/2 ounces, 100 grams) sugar

1/3 cup (2 ounces, 57 grams) milk chocolate, chopped into small chunks

1 tablespoon light corn syrup or Lyle's Golden Syrup

2 large egg whites

1/4 teaspoon cream of tartar

1 batch Oat Dough (page 17)

1 large egg

1 tablespoon water

1 cup finely ground graham cracker crumbs (about 1 sleeve of graham crackers)

I'M NOT GOING TO LIE TO YOU—these are a messy bunch of pierogies to make and fill. But s'mores are pretty sloppy in the first place, what with all that sticky marshmallow and melted chocolate. So think of these as being authentic to the real deal, and work as carefully as possible to keep everything inside the pierogi as you pinch it shut. You'll have leftover chocolate filling and marshmallow fluff, which can do double duty as sauces for the pierogies or be refrigerated for another use. Make the chocolate filling at least a day ahead so it has time to set up.

≫✿≪ ❤ ≫✿≪ ❤ ≫✿≪ ❤ ≫✿≪ ❤ ≫✿≪ ❤ ≫✿≪

Place cream and 1 tablespoon sugar in a very small saucepan over medium-low heat and whisk until sugar dissolves and cream is just starting to bubble around edges. Remove from heat. Fill another small saucepan halfway with water and bring to a simmer over medium heat. Place chocolate and corn syrup in a heatproof (stainless steel or Pyrex) bowl. Set bowl atop pan of simmering water; do not let bowl touch water. Stir until chocolate melts. Gently whisk in hot cream and continue whisking until smooth. Transfer to a clean bowl and refrigerate chocolate overnight.

Fill a small saucepan halfway with water and bring to a simmer over medium heat. Whisk egg whites and remaining 1/2 cup sugar in a heatproof (stainless steel or Pyrex) bowl. Set bowl atop pan of simmering water; do not let bowl touch water. Whisk constantly until sugar dissolves and liquid is frothy and warm to touch, 3 to 4 minutes. Remove bowl from heat. Using hand-held electric mixer on medium-high speed, beat whites until thick and glossy, 2 to 3 minutes. Add cream of tartar and continue beating until stiff peaks form, 1 to 2 minutes.

continued >

Roll out dough and stamp into rounds as directed on page 12. Place 1/4 teaspoon chilled chocolate filling on each round, then top with 1/2 teaspoon marshmallow fluff; brush with egg wash, then very carefully fold, pinch, and seal as directed. It will be messy.

If deep-frying pierogies, whisk egg and water in shallow bowl. Place graham cracker crumbs in another shallow bowl. Dip each fresh or frozen pierogi in egg wash, allowing excess to drip back into bowl, then dredge in crumbs, shaking off excess. Place on a baking sheet and deep-fry as directed on page 13.

If boiling then pan-frying pierogies, boil until softened, about 2 minutes for fresh or 3 to 4 minutes for frozen. Transfer to a baking sheet until cool enough to handle. Dip and coat pierogies as directed above and pan-fry as directed on page 13.

Serve pierogies with leftover warmed chocolate filling and marshmallow fluff if desired.

DO AHEAD: Chocolate filling can be made up to 1 week ahead and marshmallow fluff can be made up to 3 days ahead. Cover and refrigerate separately.

BLACK FOREST PIEROGIES
with Semisweet Chocolate Sauce

IN CASE THE ROSTER of recipes in this chapter hasn't made it clear, I love making jam. Just call me Joey Tribbiani, but I can't get enough of the stuff. (I also might own Thanksgiving pants, but that's another story.) This is one of the jam creations I'm most proud of—a blend that maintains its fruity cherry flavor but builds to a distinct chocolate finish. It's truly the best of both worlds.

FOR PIEROGIES: Stir cherries and sugar in a medium saucepan over medium-low heat. Cook, stirring frequently, until thickened into a sticky jam, about 20 minutes. Remove from heat. Stir in cocoa powder and vanilla bean paste. Transfer to a bowl and refrigerate at least 1 hour.

Roll out dough and stamp into rounds as directed on page 12. Place 1 teaspoon filling on each dough round; brush with egg wash, fold, pinch, and seal as directed. Deep-fry, boil, and or pan-fry pierogies as directed on page 13.

FOR SAUCE: Whisk cream and sugar in a very small saucepan over medium-low heat until sugar dissolves and cream is just starting to bubble around edges. Remove from heat. Fill a small saucepan halfway with water and bring to a simmer over medium heat. Place chocolate and corn syrup in heatproof (stainless steel or Pyrex) bowl. Set bowl atop pan of simmering water; do not let bowl touch water. Whisk to melt chocolate, then gently whisk in hot cream.

Serve pierogies with chocolate sauce.

DO AHEAD: Filling can be made up to 1 week ahead and sauce can be made up to 1 month ahead. Cover and refrigerate separately. Reheat sauce before serving.

Makes approximately 24

PIEROGIES

1 pound fresh or thawed frozen sweet cherries, pitted and coarsely chopped

$1/2$ cup ($3^{1}/2$ ounces, 100 grams) sugar

$1^{1}/2$ teaspoons unsweetened cocoa powder

1 teaspoon vanilla bean paste

1 batch Cocoa Dough (page 17)

CHOCOLATE SAUCE

$1/4$ cup heavy cream

1 tablespoon sugar

$1/3$ cup (2 ounces, 57 grams) bittersweet or semisweet chocolate, chopped into small chunks

1 tablespoon light corn syrup or Lyle's Golden Syrup

STRAWBERRY CHEESECAKE PIEROGIES

Makes approximately 24 🥟

2 tablespoons water

1¹/₂ teaspoons (¹/₂ envelope) powdered gelatin

¹/₂ cup (4 ounces, 113 grams) cream cheese, room temperature

¹/₄ cup (1 ounce, 28 grams) powdered sugar

2 tablespoons sour cream

¹/₂ pint (8 ounces, 227 grams) fresh strawberries, cut into ¹/₂-inch-wide slices

1 teaspoon packed light or dark brown sugar

¹/₈ teaspoon kosher salt

1 batch Basic Sweet Dough (page 16)

1 egg

1 tablespoon water

1 cup graham cracker crumbs (about 1 sleeve of graham crackers) or 1 cup pretzel crumbs, ground finely in a mini food processor

WHO KNEW STRAWBERRY CHEESECAKE was such an international sensation? Until I started researching this book, I was completely unaware of sernik na zimno ("cold cheesecake"), a no-bake Polish cheesecake traditionally topped with a layer of strawberry Jell-O. This, of course, got me thinking about that good old church potluck staple of strawberry-pretzel Jell-O salad, so you've got a choice here: coat your 'rogies with traditional graham cracker crumbs or go a little crazy with crushed pretzels. Your call. Make the cheesecake filling a day ahead so it has time to set up.

⚘❤ ⚘❤ ⚘❤ ⚘❤ ⚘❤ ⚘

Pour water into a small bowl. Sprinkle gelatin over and let stand for 5 minutes.

Using electric hand-held mixer on low speed, beat cream cheese, sugar, and sour cream in a bowl until light and fluffy, 2 to 3 minutes. Beat in the dissolved gelatin until fully incorporated, about 45 seconds. Cover and refrigerate overnight.

Preheat oven to 400 degrees. Line a rimmed baking sheet with parchment paper or a silicone liner. Mix strawberries with sugar and salt in a bowl, then spread in an even layer on baking sheet. Roast until strawberries have softened and slumped, releasing some of their juices, about 20 minutes. Transfer to a bowl and cool to room temperature.

Roll out dough and stamp into rounds as directed on page 12. Place 1 teaspoon filling on each dough round; top with 1 piece roasted strawberry. Brush with egg wash, fold, pinch, and seal as directed.

If deep-frying pierogies, whisk egg and water in shallow bowl. Place graham cracker crumbs or pretzel crumbs in another shallow bowl. Dip each fresh or frozen pierogi in egg wash, allowing excess to drip back into bowl, then dredge in crumbs, shaking off excess. Place on a baking sheet and deep-fry as directed on page 13.

If boiling then pan-frying pierogies, boil until softened, about 2 minutes for fresh or 3 to 4 minutes for frozen. Transfer to a baking sheet until cool enough to handle. Dip and coat pierogies as directed above and pan-fry as directed on page 13.

DO AHEAD: Cheesecake and strawberries can be made up to 2 days ahead. Cover and refrigerate separately.

POACHED PEAR PIEROGIES
with Spiced Rosé Syrup

PEARS AND I HAVE ALWAYS had an arms'-length relationship. How could they possibly compete in the flavor stakes when cranberries and citrus are around for the winter season? So I can't really explain the alchemy that occurred when I dunked 'em in rosé wine and stuffed them into pierogies, but I'm happy to report that pears and I are getting along much better after working on this recipe. It's really amazing what a glass of wine can do to improve one's outlook, eh?

Whisk wine and honey in a small to medium saucepan, then add cinnamon, peppercorns, and cloves. Add pears and bring liquid to a simmer over medium heat. Cook, stirring frequently to make sure pears are submerged, until pears are darkly translucent and liquid is reduced to deep pink syrup, 30 to 40 minutes.

Transfer pears to cutting board until cool enough to handle. Strain syrup into bowl, discarding spices. Chop pears into 1/4-inch pieces. Transfer to a bowl and refrigerate at least 1 hour.

Roll out dough and stamp into rounds as directed on page 12. Place 1 teaspoon filling on each dough round; brush with egg wash, fold, pinch, and seal as directed. Deep-fry, boil, and/or pan-fry pierogies as directed on page 13. Serve immediately with rosé syrup, either for drizzling or dipping.

DO AHEAD: Filling and syrup can be made up to 3 days ahead. Cover and refrigerate separately. Reheat rosé syrup before serving.

Makes approximately 24 🥟

2 cups dry rosé wine

1/2 cup (6 ounces, 170 grams) honey

1 cinnamon stick

1/2 teaspoon whole black peppercorns

5-6 whole cloves

1 pound ripe Bartlett pears, peeled, cored, and quartered (about 2 medium)

1 batch Basic Sweet Dough (page 16)

BLUEBERRY~LIME PIEROGIES
with Ginger Syrup

Makes approximately 24 🥟

PIEROGIES

1/2 pound (8 ounces, 227 grams) fresh blueberries

1/2 cup (3 ounces, 85 grams) coconut sugar or 1/3 cup (2 1/2 ounces, 70 grams) packed dark brown sugar

Zest of 2 small to medium limes

Juice of 2 small to medium limes

1 half-inch-thick piece of ginger, peeled and finely grated

1 batch Basic Sweet Dough (page 16)

SYRUP

1/8 pound (2 ounces, 57 grams) fresh ginger, peeled and very thinly sliced

1 cup (7 ounces, 200 grams) plus 1/4 cup (1 3/4 ounces, 50 grams) sugar

1 cup water

IF YOU'VE NEVER tasted coconut sugar before, I'm happy to introduce you to its charms in this tropically tinged recipe. Despite its name, it doesn't taste strongly of coconut, but it is earthy and complex. Try it here to see how it enhances blueberries' subtle sweetness, and I'm sure you'll find a number of excuses to start using it in other recipes (like the Tropical Fruit Salad on page 99).

❀ ♥ ❀ ♥ ❀ ♥ ❀ ♥ ❀ ♥ ❀

FOR PIEROGIES: Stir blueberries, sugar, lime zest and juice, and ginger in a small saucepan over medium-low heat. Cook, stirring frequently, until thickened into a sticky jam, about 30 to 40 minutes. Transfer to a bowl and refrigerate at least 1 hour.

Roll out dough and stamp into rounds as directed on page 12. Place 1 teaspoon filling on each dough round; brush with egg wash, fold, pinch, and seal as directed. Deep-fry, boil, and/or pan-fry pierogies as directed on page 13.

FOR SYRUP: Stir ginger slices, 1 cup sugar, and water in a small saucepan over medium heat. Bring to a simmer and cook until ginger is soft and translucent and liquid thickens to syrup, stirring occasionally, about 20 minutes. Reduce heat if liquid starts to boil and foam.

Strain syrup into a bowl. Toss ginger slices with remaining 1/4 cup sugar in a separate bowl; dry slices on a wire rack to crystallize into candied ginger.

Serve pierogies with ginger syrup and candied ginger.

DO AHEAD: Filling, syrup, and candied ginger can be made up to 1 week ahead. Cover and refrigerate separately. Reheat syrup before serving.

PICKLED STRAWBERRY JAM PIEROGIES
with White Chocolate Sauce

YOU MIGHT BE WEIRDED OUT by seeing the words "pickled" and "strawberries" in the same sentence, but trust me, you're looking at a winning combination. The jam is tangy but not sour, and just different enough to hook you with a single bite.

FOR PIEROGIES: Bring vinegars, peppercorns, and star anise to a boil in a very small saucepan over medium-low heat. Remove from heat; cover and let steep 30 minutes.

Strain vinegar into a medium saucepan; discard spices. Whisk sugar, pectin, and salt in a bowl, then whisk into vinegar. Add strawberries and stir over medium-high heat until sugar dissolves and mixture starts to bubble. Reduce heat and cook, stirring frequently, until thickened into a sticky jam, 35 to 45 minutes. Transfer to a bowl and refrigerate at least 1 hour.

Roll out dough and stamp into rounds as directed on page 12. Place 1 teaspoon filling on each dough round; brush with egg wash, fold, pinch, and seal as directed. Deep-fry, boil, and/or pan-fry pierogies as directed on page 13.

FOR SAUCE: Fill a small saucepan halfway with water and bring to a simmer over medium heat. Place chocolate, cream, and corn syrup in a heatproof (stainless steel or Pyrex) bowl. Set bowl atop pan of simmering water; do not let bowl touch water. Stir mixture constantly to melt chocolate.

Serve pierogies with chocolate sauce, either for drizzling or dipping.

DO AHEAD: Filling can be made up to 1 week ahead and sauce can be made up to 1 month ahead. Cover and refrigerate separately. Reheat sauce before serving.

Makes approximately 24 🥟

PIEROGIES

1/4 cup Champagne vinegar

1 tablespoon sherry vinegar

1/2 teaspoon whole black peppercorns

1/4 teaspoon Szechuan peppercorns

1/2 whole star anise pod

1/2 cup (3 1/2 ounces, 100 grams) sugar

1 tablespoon powdered low-sugar pectin

1 teaspoon kosher salt

1 pound (1 dry pint) strawberries, cut into small pieces

1 batch Basic Sweet Dough (page 16)

SAUCE

2/3 cup (4 ounces, 113 grams) white chocolate, chopped into small pieces

1/4 cup heavy cream

1 tablespoon light corn syrup or Lyle's Golden Syrup

PEACH CRUMBLE PIEROGIES

Makes approximately 24 🥟

PIEROGIES

¹/₂ pound (8 ounces, 227 grams) fresh peaches
(about 2 medium to large)

2 tablespoons packed light brown sugar

¹/₂ teaspoon vanilla bean paste

¹/₄ teaspoon ground allspice

1 tablespoon cornstarch

1 tablespoon water

1 batch Oat Dough or Whole-Wheat Dough
(page 17)

IT'S MY SUMMER BREAKFAST RITUAL: standing over the sink, devouring a fresh peach, no plate necessary. In the height of peach season I can plow through two pounds a week this way without even thinking of saving a few for a cobbler or pie. But because all things must end, I've stashed a few dozen of these in my freezer to remind me of warm-weather days. The crumble topping freezes incredibly well, too—spread it on a baking sheet as you would pierogies and transfer to a bag once it's hard.

❧ ✿ ❧ ♥ ❧ ✿ ❧ ♥ ❧ ✿ ❧ ♥ ❧ ✿ ❧ ♥ ❧ ✿ ❧ ♥ ❧ ✿ ❧

FOR PIEROGIES: Fill a small deep saucepan with water and bring to a boil. Fill a large bowl with ice water. Using a paring knife, slice an x in top and bottom of each peach. Submerge peach in boiling water until skin loosens, 30 to 45 seconds. Transfer peach from water to ice bath. Repeat with remaining peaches. Remove skins, then coarsely chop peaches.

Discard water from saucepan and stir peaches, sugar, vanilla bean paste, and allspice in pan. Cook over medium-low heat, stirring frequently, until thickened into a sticky jam, 10 to 15 minutes.

Whisk cornstarch and water in a bowl. Whisk into peaches and cook 1 minute. Transfer to a bowl and refrigerate at least 1 hour.

Roll out dough and stamp into rounds as directed on page 12. Place 1 teaspoon filling on each dough round; brush with egg wash, fold, pinch, and seal as directed. Deep-fry, boil, and/or pan-fry pierogies as directed on page 13.

continued >

TOPPING

1/2 cup (3 3/4 ounces, 106 grams) packed light brown sugar

1/2 cup (2 1/8 ounces, 60 grams) unbleached all-purpose flour

1/4 cup chopped pecans

1/4 cup quick rolled oats (nut-allergic folks, omit pecans and use 1/2 cup oats)

1/4 teaspoon ground allspice

1/4 teaspoon freshly grated nutmeg

1/4 teaspoon kosher salt

4 tablespoons (2 ounces, 57 grams) unsalted butter, cut into 1/2-inch cubes, room temperature

FOR TOPPING: Preheat oven to 375 degrees. Line a rimmed baking sheet with foil or parchment paper. Whisk brown sugar, flour, pecans, oats, allspice, nutmeg, and salt in a bowl. Add butter and blend in with fingers until mixture is moist and crumbly. Spread in an even layer on baking sheet. Bake until crisp and golden brown, about 15 minutes. Cool to room temperature.

Generously sprinkle the crumble topping over pierogies and serve.

DO AHEAD: Filling can be made up to 2 days ahead and topping can be made up to 1 week ahead. Cover and refrigerate separately or freeze topping for up to 6 months.

APRICOT, ROSEMARY, AND PINE NUT PIEROGIES

IN A WORLD WHERE SUPERMARKETS showcase thick stubs of asparagus and incongruous cobs of corn even in the dead of winter, apricots remain stubbornly seasonal. Good luck trying to find one in the Northeast in January, at least. That gives this recipe a fleeting but sublime window of opportunity: Make it when apricots are ripe and intoxicatingly fragrant. They'll be so sweet the jam will practically dissolve into itself, so take care not to burn it.

❧ ❀ ❧ ❀ ❧ ❀ ❧ ❀ ❧ ❀ ❧ ❀ ❧ ❀

Stir apricots, sugar, and $1/4$ teaspoon rosemary in a small saucepan over low heat. Cook, stirring frequently, until thickened into a sticky jam, about 10 minutes. Transfer to a bowl and refrigerate at least 1 hour.

Stir pine nuts into filling.

Make a batch of dough, whisking remaining $1/4$ teaspoon rosemary in with the flour. Roll out dough and stamp into rounds as directed on page 12. Place 1 teaspoon filling on each dough round; brush with egg wash, fold, pinch, and seal as directed. Deep-fry, boil, and/or pan-fry pierogies as directed on page 13.

DO AHEAD: Filling can be made up to 1 week ahead. Cover and refrigerate.

Makes approximately 24

$1/2$ pound (8 ounces, 227 grams) fresh apricots (about 2 to 3 small to medium), coarsely chopped

2 tablespoons sugar

$1/2$ teaspoon minced fresh rosemary, divided in half

1 heaping tablespoon ($1/2$ ounce, 14 grams) pine nuts, toasted and chopped

1 batch Basic Sweet Dough (page 16)

CHERRY-ALMOND PIEROGIES

Makes approximately 24 🥟

1/2 pound (8 ounces, 227 grams) fresh or thawed frozen sweet cherries, pitted and quartered

1/4 cup amaretto liqueur

2 tablespoons (1/2 ounce, 14 grams) finely chopped roasted almonds

1/4 teaspoon almond or orange extract (optional)

1 batch Basic Sweet Dough (page 16)

IF YOU'RE THE CANNING and preserving type, you might know that stone fruit pits, like those from cherries or apricots, can be used to make homemade amaretto liqueur. And if you want to use the pits from the sweet cherries in this recipe to make the liqueur that flavors this jam, be my guest—but I'm the impatient type and would rather just buy a nice bottle of amaretto for my immediate gratification. There's also no law saying the cook can't sip on a little amaretto while she makes these pierogies . . . just saying.

❧ ❦ ❧ ❦ ❧ ❦ ❧ ❦ ❧ ❦ ❧ ❦

Bring cherries and amaretto to a simmer in a small saucepan over medium-low heat. Cook until cherries are soft and syrupy and liquid is mostly absorbed, stirring occasionally, 20 to 25 minutes. Stir in almonds and extract if desired. Transfer to a bowl and refrigerate at least 1 hour.

Roll out dough and stamp into rounds as directed on page 12. Place 1 teaspoon filling on each dough round; brush with egg wash, fold, pinch, and seal as directed. Deep-fry, boil, and/or pan-fry pierogies as directed on page 13.

DO AHEAD: Filling can be made up to 3 days ahead. Cover and refrigerate.

ROASTED GRANNY SMITH APPLE AND BRIE PIEROGIES

OH, COME ON, you might roll your eyes at the old-school baked brie in phyllo pastry appetizer . . . but you know you're not too cool to snag one every time you see it making the rounds at every wedding you've ever been to in your life. So what's stopping you from making this little number, with spicy-sweet apples nestled in there to boot?

≫✿≪ ❤ ≫✿≪ ❤ ≫✿≪ ❤ ≫✿≪ ❤ ≫✿≪ ❤ ≫✿≪

Preheat oven to 400 degrees. Place butter in an 8-inch square baking dish and heat in oven until butter melts. Remove dish from oven and stir in sugar, ginger, cayenne, and mace until sugar dissolves. Toss apple cubes in spiced butter. Roast until apples are soft and starting to caramelize but still hold their shape, stirring occasionally, 20 to 30 minutes.

Roll out dough and stamp into rounds as directed on page 12. Place 1 cheese square on each dough round, then top with 1 teaspoon apples; brush with egg wash, fold, pinch, and seal as directed. Deep-fry, boil, and/or pan-fry pierogies as directed on page 13.

DO AHEAD: Apples can be cooked up to 2 days ahead. Cover and refrigerate.

Makes approximately 24 🥟

1 tablespoon unsalted butter

1 tablespoon packed light or dark brown sugar

$1/2$ teaspoon ground ginger

$1/4$ teaspoon cayenne

$1/4$ teaspoon ground mace or nutmeg

$1/2$ pound (8 ounces, 227 grams) Granny Smith apple (about 1 medium), peeled, cored, and diced into $1/2$-inch cubes

1 batch Basic Sweet Dough (page 16)

$1/4$ pound (4 ounces, 113 grams) Brie or Camembert cheese, sliced into $1/2$-inch squares

CRANBERRY GINGERBREAD PIEROGIES

I JUST DON'T UNDERSTAND how people go off their rockers for pumpkin spice treats every autumn while the glorious spicy taste of gingerbread gets taken for granted every holiday season. Gingerbread has so much more depth and nuance, thanks to that sultry touch of molasses that makes all the difference. Making a holiday-inspired pierogi had been on my list from day one of working on this book, and I hope I've done it justice here.

》❀《 ♥ 》❀《 ♥ 》❀《 ♥ 》❀《 ♥ 》❀《 ♥ 》❀《

Combine cranberries and water in a small saucepan and bring to a boil over medium heat. Cook until cranberries start to pop and soften, stirring frequently. When cranberries are mostly liquefied, add maple syrup and continue cooking, stirring frequently, until thickened into a sticky jam, 15 to 20 minutes. Reduce heat if bubbling too much. Transfer to a bowl and refrigerate at least 1 hour.

Make a batch of dough with the following changes: Whisk cinnamon, ginger, and allspice with oat and all-purpose flours in a bowl. Reduce 3 tablespoons butter to 2 tablespoons. Replace sugar with brown sugar, and whisk brown sugar and molasses in with egg, sour cream, butter, and salt.

Roll out dough and stamp into rounds as directed on page 12. Place 1 teaspoon filling on each dough round; brush with egg wash, fold, pinch, and seal as directed. Deep-fry, boil, and/or pan-fry pierogies as directed on page 13. Serve sprinkled with powdered sugar or cinnamon sugar if desired.

DO AHEAD: Filling can be made up to 1 week ahead. Cover and refrigerate.

Makes approximately 24 🥟

2 cups (7 ounces, 198 grams) fresh or thawed frozen cranberries

1/4 cup water

1/4 cup dark maple syrup

1 batch Oat Dough (page 17)

1/2 teaspoon ground cinnamon

1/2 teaspoon ground ginger

1/2 teaspoon ground allspice or cloves

1 tablespoon packed dark brown sugar

1 tablespoon molasses

Powdered sugar or cinnamon sugar (optional)

SWEET POTATO PIE~ROGIES
with Pecan Praline and Toasted Marshmallow Fluff

Makes approximately 24

PIEROGIES

$1/3$ cup ($2^{1}/3$ ounces, 66 grams) sugar

$1/4$ cup ($1^{7}/8$ ounces, 53 grams) plus 3 tablespoons packed dark brown sugar

$1/4$ cup whole or reduced-fat milk

$1/8$ teaspoon kosher salt

$1/8$ teaspoon baking soda

4 tablespoons (2 ounces, 57 grams) unsalted butter, divided in half

$1/2$ cup (2 ounces, 57 grams) toasted whole pecans

1 cup (8 ounces, 227 grams) sweet potato puree

1 teaspoon vanilla bean paste

$1/4$ teaspoon ground cinnamon

$1/4$ teaspoon freshly grated nutmeg

1 batch Basic Sweet Dough or Oat Dough (pages 16–17)

OK, RIDDLE ME THIS: why does sweet potato pie beat the pants off pumpkin pie in my personal taste sweepstakes? The logical explanation is that sweet potato pie is lighter and fluffier, but the more fun (and tastier) hypothesis is that there always seems to be some sort of pecan-related topping or accessory involved. Add a dollop of fresh, homemade marshmallow fluff to the mix? Yeah, that's the ticket.

❦❀❦ ♥ ❦❀❦ ♥ ❦❀❦ ♥ ❦❀❦ ♥ ❦❀❦ ♥ ❦❀❦

FOR PIEROGIES: Line a baking sheet with parchment paper or a silicone liner. Whisk sugar, $1/4$ cup brown sugar, milk, salt, and baking soda in a small high-sided saucepan. Add 2 tablespoons butter and stir over medium heat until sugar dissolves and butter melts. Bring to a boil and clip a candy thermometer to pan. Continue to cook without stirring until thermometer registers 240 degrees; mixture will be densely foamy. Remove thermometer and stir in pecans. Quickly and carefully scrape pecan praline onto baking sheet, spreading as evenly as you can, since it hardens almost instantly. Let praline cool to room temperature.

Melt remaining 2 tablespoons butter in a small saucepan over medium-low heat. Whisk in remaining 3 tablespoons brown sugar and cook until sugar dissolves and mixture resembles caramel sauce, whisking constantly, 2 to 3 minutes. Scrape into a bowl. Add sweet potato puree, vanilla bean paste, cinnamon, and nutmeg. Finely chop about half the pecan praline and add to sweet potato filling. (Reserve remaining praline for another use, or eat it yourself.)

continued >

MARSHMALLOW FLUFF

1 large egg white

1/4 cup (1 3/4 ounces, 50 grams) sugar

1/8 teaspoon cream of tartar

Roll out dough and stamp into rounds as directed on page 12. Place 1 teaspoon filling on each dough round; brush with egg wash, fold, pinch, and seal as directed. Deep-fry, boil, and/or pan-fry pierogies as directed on page 13.

FOR MARSHMALLOW FLUFF: Fill a small saucepan halfway with water and bring to a simmer over medium heat. Whisk egg white and sugar in a heatproof (stainless steel or Pyrex) bowl. Set bowl atop pan of simmering water; do not let bowl touch water. Whisk constantly until sugar dissolves and liquid is frothy and warm to touch, 2 to 3 minutes. Remove bowl from heat. Using hand-held electric mixer on medium-high speed, beat whites until thick and glossy, 1 to 2 minutes. Add cream of tartar and continue beating until stiff peaks form, 1 to 2 minutes.

Preheat broiler. Line a baking sheet with parchment paper or a silicone liner. Arrange cooked pierogies on baking sheet. Top each pierogi with a dollop of marshmallow fluff. Broil until marshmallow fluff browns, watching closely, about 1 minute. Alternatively, use a culinary torch to brown marshmallow. Serve immediately.

DO AHEAD: Praline and filling can be made 3 days ahead. Cover and store praline at room temperature. Cover and refrigerate filling.

ACKNOWLEDGMENTS

To Tessa, who helped me brainstorm the initial idea for this book over a round of beers, hot dogs, and pierogies at Franktuary and refined the idea over cocktails and more pierogies at Butterjoint;

To Dan, who dutifully sampled more than his share of pierogies (though I'm not sure testing the Caramello version was a hardship) and gave up ice cream for months to allocate every inch of freezer space to pierogi storage;

To Rebecca Peters-Golden, Mamata Reddy, Matt Rolak, and Amanda Whitehead, my harshly overworked but still devoted band of recipe testers, who became just as fanatical about pierogies as I hope every reader will be;

To Liz Tarpy, the best photo and food styling assistant a gal could hope for;

To Andrea Lynn, my voice of reason and partner in insanity;

To my parents, for having the foresight to raise me in western PA;

To Clare Pelino, for immediately getting enthusiastic about this book and for sharing that first Daisy Cutter with me in Chicago;

To Madge Baird and the rest of the Gibbs Smith team for producing such a beautiful book;

To Jenny Lewis and Taylor Swift, for providing excellent soundtracks for pierogi-making;

To the Pittsburgh Pirates, for keeping the faith and the pierogi love alive;

And to everyone who chimed in with excitement and anticipation for this book. I knew pierogi pride was strong throughout the U.S., but I didn't realize how much passion these little dumplings inspired until now.

Thanks to all of yinz.

ABOUT THE AUTHOR

Casey Barber is a freelance food writer and photographer, editor of the online magazine *Good. Food. Stories.* (goodfoodstories. com), and the author of *Classic Snacks Made from Scratch: 70 Homemade Versions of Your Favorite Brand-Name Treats*. Though she'll always be a Pittsburgher at heart, Casey lives in northern New Jersey with her husband, two cats, and a freezer full of kielbasa, sour cherries . . . and pierogies. Learn more about Casey at caseybarber.com.